Cox's Book of Modern Saints and Martyrs

Caroline Cox
(The Baroness Cox)
with
Catherine Butcher

continuum
LONDON • NEW YORK

Continuum

The Tower Building
11 York Road
London SE1 7NX

80 Maiden Lane
Suite 704
New York NY 10038

www.continuumbooks.com

First published 2006

British Library Cataloguing-in-Publication Data
A catalogue record for this book is available from the British Library.

ISBN 0 8264 8788 2

Typeset by Kenneth Burnley, Wirral, Cheshire
Printed and bound in Great Britain by MPG Books Ltd, Bodmin, Cornwall

Contents

Contents

Contents

Contents

Acknowledgements

First and foremost, thanks are due to all those whose stories we include in this book. We owe a debt of heartfelt gratitude for the privilege of meeting some of the contemporary saints whose stories we tell, as well as paying our profound respect to the martyrs whose faithful witness unto death is recorded in these pages.

We are also grateful for help from the following:

Carolyn Armitage, Continuum
Michael Bourdeaux, Keston Institute
Anastasia Dubovik, Barnabas Fund
Nina Kelly, Press Relations, Open Doors
Tina Lambert, Christian Solidarity Worldwide
Jana Pearson, Personal Assistant to Baroness Cox
Davorin Peterlin, Director, Keston Institute
Peter Riddell, Centre for Islamic Studies, London
    School of Theology
Benedict Rogers, Christian Solidarity Worldwide
Nancy von Schimmelmann, Compass Direct
Jeff Sellers, Managing Editor, Compass Direct
Ann Shukman, Keston Institute
Geoffrey Smith, Christian Friends of Israel
Patrick Sookhdeo, Barnabas Fund
Lauri Sturges-Cobb, Fieldstead Institute
Andrew Walby, Continuum
Malcolm Walker, Librarian, Keston Institute
Wilfred Wong, Jubilee Campaign
Dan Wooding, Assist Ministries
Sam Yeghnazar, Elam Ministries

Acknowledgements

We are also grateful to those organizations whose research and publications have been invaluable. Sources from which we have derived much valuable information include:

Assist News
Barnabas Fund
Compass Direct
CSW
Elam Ministries
Jubilee Campaign
Keston Institute
Open Doors

Foreword

It is with a sense of deep humility and gratitude that I take this opportunity of paying tribute to the saints and martyrs of the Christian Church throughout the years and throughout the world. Some of these are remembered and spoken of all over the world; the names of others are forgotten except by their immediate family and friends. But all are known to God, and all have made an indelible mark in the story of the gospel of our Lord Jesus Christ.

Inevitably it is those whom we have known most closely whose lives and deaths affect us most deeply, and therefore I must pay particular tribute to those who have been martyred in Nigeria, including the Revd Bitrus Manjang, the Revd Iyasco Taru, and Evangelist Mrs Jinkai. I personally have lost classmates, colleagues and friends in this way. This has had a huge effect upon my life. My family and I lost all our possessions in the fire of persecution, but we are still alive. I find myself pondering on this and asking why it should be so.

One result is that my focus has been sharpened. It is a matter of urgency for us to preach and live out the gospel in truth and in love, so that if we are taken by death through persecution we will have fulfilled our mission on earth. It is essential that we live each day for the Lord, as we do not know the time or the place that our lives may be required of us. Physical death is a reality. Spiritual death is also a reality. The latter is caused by lack of faith – lack of faith in the word of God, lack of faith in the power of God, and lack of faith in the power of the Holy Spirit to enable us to live for God in this life and to spread the good news of the gospel to others in mission.

Foreword

Physical death need not of course come as a result of persecution, but those who have died in this way put before us both a challenge and an inspiration. Why should this be so? How can a person accept death for faith in Christ and for living the gospel? We may not know our own answer until we are tested, and it may be that testing is necessary for the strengthening of our faith.

As we pray for those who are suffering persecution now, let us all flee from spiritual death by committing our lives to the Lord Jesus Christ, so that whenever and however physical death appears, we may be counted as faithful servants, called through his grace to enter the kingdom of God.

Blessed be the God and Father of our Lord Jesus Christ, who according to His great mercy has caused us to be born again to a living hope through the resurrection of Jesus Christ from the dead, to obtain an inheritance which is imperishable and undefiled and will not fade away, reserved in heaven for you, who are protected by the power of God through faith for a salvation ready to be revealed in the last time.

In this you greatly rejoice, even though now for a little while, if necessary, you have been distressed by various trials, so that the proof of your faith, being more precious than gold which is perishable, even though tested by fire, may be found to result in praise and glory and honor at the revelation of Jesus Christ. (1 Peter 1:3–7, New American Standard Bible)

✠ Rt Revd Dr Benjamin A. Kwashi
Bishop of the Anglican diocese of Jos,
Plateau State, Nigeria

Introduction

Some four hundred years ago, John Foxe wrote his famous book documenting the stories of martyrs. Since then, countless men, women and children have chosen to die for their Christian faith. Many are still making that choice. It has been one of the greatest privileges of my life to meet some of these contemporary Christians who are living 'on the edge', constantly prepared to make the ultimate sacrifice. I always return from my visits humbled and inspired beyond words by their courage, dignity, love and what I can only call 'miracles of grace'.

It is important for their stories to be told, for many reasons. The testimonies of modern martyrs should be recorded and celebrated – not consigned to the dustbin of history. And the witness of those who could become martyrs in our lifetime should be available for all to appreciate.

Foxe's Book of Martyrs, with its harrowing details of martyrdom, is not an easy read. However, these stories, although they challenge us with their accounts of almost incredible fortitude and endurance, are not morbid or depressing. They are infused with indomitable hope, often with indescribable joy and with a peace which the tribulations of this world cannot destroy.

It is our hope that this book will provide a rich resource of spiritual encounters. Obviously, there are many other people who could have been included. But those whose stories are recounted here are examples of all who, in our lifetime, have accepted, or are prepared to accept, martyrdom. Their witness may serve as a source of inspiration for personal meditation, for sermons and Sunday schools, or for religious education and worship in schools. For here in this book is evidence of a faith which transcends doctrinaire divisions and a love which reflects the love of Christ who came to die for all, that all may live.

Introduction

Inevitable questions arise about definitions. We define as Christian 'martyrs' those who have deliberately chosen the possibility of death in their refusal to compromise their way of life and their witness to their Christian faith – and who have paid the price with their lives. We define as 'saints' those who constantly face the possibility of martyrdom; some may well be martyred in our lifetime.

We hope that readers will go to visit a number of these men and women whom we define as contemporary saints. Those who make this effort will be inspired beyond measure by a living witness and commitment to a faith which is so precious that people are prepared to lay down their lives for it. Such encounters may help us, who live in freedom without suffering the costs of persecution, to appreciate the privileges we have and to remember that from those to whom much is given, much is required.

While focusing on Christianity, we readily acknowledge that there are many people with other faiths and beliefs who demonstrate in their lives qualities comparable in many ways to those described in this book. We honour them and do not wish to imply that such inspiring stories are the prerogative of Christianity. However, we have such an abundance of testimonies of men, women and children within the Christian tradition whose stories need to be recorded that we have had to be painfully, and to some extent arbitrarily, selective. This selection reflects the areas in which I have had personal contact. We hope that this will be volume one. A subsequent volume – or volumes – will give further opportunities to celebrate the faith of other contemporary saints and martyrs. We would rejoice if more books would be written, within the Christian Church and also from other faith traditions, which remind us that there are men, women and children around the world who inspire us by their witness and commitment to the ultimate values of love and truth.

In the meantime, we hope this book may also serve as a challenge to 'comfortable Christianity', prompting the church in the West to put issues which currently divide and distract us into perspective. St Paul, in his letter to the church in Corinth, reminded us: 'When one part of the Body of Christ suffers, we all suffer.' Do we? The contemporary Christians who are suffering affliction for their faith or are also suffering for our faith, if we call ourselves Christians. They do so uncomplainingly and often joyfully. But they do ask for our prayers. We trust that this book may help to promote a wider, deeper intercessory support for the persecuted church.

We also hope that it may challenge each of us to consider how we should respond, individually, collectively and prayerfully, to those forces which are causes of contemporary persecution and oppression. In many parts of the world, Christians are valiantly holding to the faith, often inspite of seemingly overwhelming odds. They need our help and support. As St Teresa of Avila reminds us, God has no hands or voice but ours. If we look the other way, if we remain silent, the Church in many places may be overwhelmed in our time. Already in parts of Turkey and the Middle East, historic churches are being reduced to empty ruins or crumbling monasteries where ageing monks spend their final years. As Christians, we believe that the blood of the martyrs is the seed of the Church. But that does not exonerate us from playing our part in supporting those who are trying to sustain a living Church against formidable odds on the frontiers of faith – and who are often paying with their lives to do so.

> By the light of burning martyrs,
> Christ, thy bleeding feet we track,
> Toiling up new Calvaries ever
> With the Cross that turns not back.
> New occasions teach new duties;
> Time makes ancient good uncouth;
> They must upward still and onward
> Who would keep abreast of truth.
> James Russell Lowell (1819–1891)

This book is dedicated to those who are now experiencing their Gethsemanes and enduring their Calvaries. As Christians, we know that, while we can join with Mary in contemplation as she stood at the foot of the cross, with profound grief, we can also rejoice in the love of Christ incarnate, who is our risen Lord. This does not exonerate us from supporting his contemporary

3

Introduction

followers who are living and dying for Him. But it does transform their stories from morbid tales of tribulation into testimonies
of lives which shine with the light of indomitable faith in a God
of redemptive love. He is manifestly with them throughout their
trials. He also calls us, who call ourselves Christians, to his service,
whoever and wherever we are.

Caroline Cox

Pray for the Church

Pray for the Church, afflicted and oppressed.
For all who suffer for the Gospel's sake,
That Christ may show us how to serve them best
In that one kingdom Satan cannot shake.
But how much more than us they have to give,
Who by their dying show us how to live.

Pray for Christ's dissidents, who daily wait,
As Jesus waited in the olive grove,
The unjust trial, the pre-determined fate,
The world's contempt for reconciling love.
Shall all they won for us, at such a cost,
Be by our negligence or weakness lost?

Pray that if times of testing should lay bare
What sort we are, who call ourselves His own,
We may be counted worthy then to wear,
With quiet fortitude, Christ's only crown:
The crown of thorns that in His saints He wears again –
The crown of thorns that signifies His reign.

Frederick Pratt Green (1903–2000)

Asia

I

A modern-day child martyr

Roy Pontoh (1984–1999), Ambon, Indonesia

Ambon used to be a beautiful town in the exotic Spice Islands of Indonesia, until 1999, when it became the epicentre of a violent conflict between Muslim and Christian communities which was to cause the deaths of thousands.

I was visiting the region as part of a group taking medical aid and promoting reconciliation when I met a young boy who told me this sobering, challenging and inspiring story. He is remembering the death of his best friend, Roy, aged fifteen, as he describes in chilling detail the events he witnessed on 20 January 1999.

The youth group from our church had gone away for a Bible study camping weekend. We were having a very happy time until the terrible moment when a group of Muslim jihad warriors came looking for us. They took my friend Roy aside and one of the jihad warriors asked him, 'Who are you?'

'I am a soldier of Christ!' Roy replied. The man who asked the question struck Roy with his machete, almost severing his left arm.

The man repeated the question: 'Who are you?' Again, Roy replied: 'I am one of Christ's soldiers.'

The jihad warrior struck Roy with his machete a second time, leaving a big gash on the boy's right shoulder.

The warrior then asked the question a third time. Although he was in agony, Roy's response began respectfully: 'Uncle – I cannot say anything else – I am a soldier for Christ.' The next swing of the machete ripped open Roy's stomach. Roy shouted: 'Jesuusss!!' As he dropped to his knees, the executioner slit open the boy's throat. Roy was martyred.

As I talk to this boy describing the martyrdom of his friend, I am deeply humbled – not only by Roy's faithfulness in the face of death, but by the demeanour of his friend. His face is so serene that I have no doubt that, in a similar situation, he would do precisely what his best friend had done. And perhaps the most humbling aspect of the whole scene was that it seemed as if this momentous event was no 'big deal'. This is the price they expect to pay for our faith – the child martyrs of our day.

Each of the accounts of persecution and martyrdom in this book is true. We have sought to let the facts speak for themselves, wherever possible using eyewitness accounts or people's own words.

To verify the facts of Roy Pontoh's martyrdom, Open Doors workers also visited Ambon and gathered almost everybody who was within fifteen metres of Roy when he was martyred, including Roy's older nephew, who was only five metres away from Roy during the last minutes of his life. Others present were a couple of his close friends, Roy's pastor, and other young people who survived the attack. These witnesses explained to Open Doors that Roy Pontoh was among 125 mostly Christian children and teenagers from the New Covenant Christian Church (GKPB). They had gathered for a Bible camp at the Station Field Complex of Pattimura University at Hila, on the island of Ambon. The theme of their time together was 'God's Army'.

When the camp was over, several of the leaders drove to the local military post (Koramil) at Hitu village to seek protection for the children who were waiting for rides home, because of the dangerous conditions in the area. Roy's youth pastor, Meiky Sainyakit, and three other Christian men, one a police officer, failed to get any assistance from the military, so they headed back to the camp. On their way, the men were attacked by a Muslim mob in the village of Wakal. They were pulled from their vehicle onto the road. Meiky Sainyakit and the driver were stabbed to death, and later their bodies were burned by the mob. A third man, Henry Kursepuny, escaped death when he was rescued by a retired policeman.

Around 2 p.m., Muslim extremists and Laskar Jihad fighters

from the surrounding villages began to converge in front of the university's gate. The children could tell that the crowd was growing as the shouts and chanting were getting louder and louder.

One of the fathers whose children attended the camp looked nervously at one of the older teenagers and said, 'The Muslims are coming. We'd better hide the kids.' Others, following his lead, helped the smaller children find hiding places in the many rooms in the complex, such as the classrooms, the bathrooms, and the kitchen. Then they hid themselves and prayed hard.

Around 4 p.m., the mob finally burst into the complex with machetes, spears, knives, and clubs. They found many of the teenagers, forced them to come out of hiding, and began beating them mercilessly. Roy Pontoh was among those who were discovered. Separated from the group, they were herded into the main dining room and assaulted with beatings and insults. Roy was beaten several times. Then all the girls and women were separated and forced out of the building, leaving the boys and men, and the assailants.

Roy Pontoh was dragged from the group, questioned and killed by the jihad warrior with a machete, as Roy's friend described to me later. The mob then dragged Roy's body out and threw it in a ditch along with another victim, Hermanus Chursam. Two more bodies were discovered later in the compound, by Henky Pattiwael and one of the complex's workers, Bung Karel. Three days later, the bodies of Roy and the others were recovered by Heri Latuheru and some police officers.

Roy's parents heard from eyewitnesses of their son's last testimony of bravery. Although grief-stricken, they are proud of their son, who stood strong in his faith to the end.

We might be tempted to think that such persecution and martyrdom only occurs in contexts like this. But Roy Pontoh's martyrdom is not an isolated Indonesian incident. I have been privileged to meet many Christians around the world who live with the daily possibility of martyrdom. Despite living with dangers and deprivations of many kinds, they are often full of joy, humour – and that peace which the world can neither give nor take away.

Chapter 2
Peace like a river

[B]ut we also rejoice in our sufferings, because we know that suffering produces perseverance; perseverance, character; and character, hope. And hope does not disappoint us, because God has poured out his love into our hearts by the Holy Spirit, whom he has given us.

(Romans 5:3–5, New International Version)

Indonesia has had a turbulent history: colonized by the Dutch in the early seventeenth century; occupied by Japan from 1942 to 1945; subject to the autocratic rule of President Sukarno, and under the equally dictatorial rule of General Suharto, from 1967 until 1989; then struggling to move towards democracy, with Indonesia's first direct presidential election in 2004.

Central Sulawesi is one of Indonesia's six provinces. I travelled there in 2003 to attend the trial of Reverend Damanik.

Rinaldy Damanik (b. 1960), Central Sulawesi, Indonesia

I first met the Revd Rinaldy Damanik in 2003 in a hot, bare prison cell in Palu, Central Sulawesi. I had gone to this beautiful but conflict-scarred island to demonstrate international interest in Revd Damanik's trial, scheduled for the next morning. Many people, myself included, believed that this man was innocent. Damanik has risked his life many times rescuing people caught up in widespread violence in which many hundreds have perished during militant Muslim attacks on Christian and Hindu communities and subsequent counterattacks. His crisis centre earned a reputation for aiding victims of violence, Christian and Muslim alike. He had also been very active in trying to promote reconciliation between the communities.

In August 2002, Damanik and his team were evacuating Christians from a village that had recently been attacked, when their vehicles were stopped by an angry Muslim mob. In an apparent attempt to placate the mob, the police arrived and made a show of searching the cars. The next day, much to everyone's surprise, the police announced that the search had discovered illegal weapons.

This incident was generally believed to have been contrived to frame Damanik by those who did not want peace and reconciliation. His accusers could not even agree on the number of weapons allegedly removed from the vehicles, but he was arrested on 11 September and sent to prison.

It was now seven months after his arrest. As I entered his dingy cell, my first impression was of a man with a joyful, warm smile, who radiated happiness and love. He told me that he had been offered freedom if he would plead guilty but said he could not accept freedom on that false premise.

The next morning, I met the judges, explaining that my presence was not meant to indicate any interference in the internal affairs of Indonesia. However, I and my colleagues hoped we would be able to report to the international community that the judges would demonstrate a commitment to justice, the rule of law, due process and the principles of democracy and civil society which Indonesia is striving to achieve.

In the hot, sultry courtroom, I had a seat in the front row. Just in front of me stood Rinaldy Damanik, alone, defenceless – except for the defence of the truth. He addressed the three judges seated on the platform above him:

> Your Honours, I have been offered my freedom if I will plead guilty. But that I cannot do, because I am not guilty. I cannot accept freedom on the basis of a lie. We cannot build the future for our children, for our grandchildren, for Indonesia on the basis of a lie. Even if I must spend many years in prison

even if I must go to the scaffold, I would prefer to go to the scaffold for the truth than to accept freedom for a lie.

Sitting so close to this brave man who accepted the possibility of death on a scaffold for the truth, this verse from one of my favourite hymns kept going through my mind, again and again:

> Though the cause of evil prosper,
> Yet 'tis truth alone is strong;
> Though her portion be the scaffold,
> And upon the throne be wrong –
> Yet that scaffold sways the future,
> And, behind the dim unknown,
> Standeth God within the shadow,
> Keeping watch above his own.
>
> James Russell Lowell (1819–1891)

A key prosecution witness in Damanik's trial, Sartob Sambegewe, said that he had been beaten by the police and that his written statement implicating Damanik was a product of police brutality; but this testimony was simply disregarded by the court. The police officers called as witnesses for the prosecution gave contradictory testimony regarding which vehicle Damanik was in and whether he was a passenger or a driver.

Despite these and numerous other irregularities Rinaldy Damanik was found guilty and given a three-year prison sentence.

The next time I saw him was in November 2005 in England, in the House of Lords. He had been released several months early. He attributes this to international prayer and also to pressure on the Indonesian authorities. He greets me with the same radiant, warm, joyful smile I remember so well from the time I met him in prison. His first words were: 'When you came to that prison, it was like a miracle – that someone from the West, a politician, should care enough to come . . .'

Over tea in the elegant surroundings of Parliament, he recounts some of his experiences.

He was born in Medan, North Sulawesi on 9 September

1960. He attended school in Medan and went on to study at the Faculty of Technology in the University of North Sumatra. Then 'God touched my heart', he said. He changed his mind, left the university and transferred to theological college in Southern Sulawesi. He was sponsored by the Christian Churches of Central Sulawesi and he subsequently went to work in Tentena. When he was arrested, he was working as Head of the Crisis Centre, a humanitarian aid and human rights organization serving all the churches – both Protestant and Roman Catholic.

He recalls some of his experiences in prison, prefacing his stories with praise to God, who gave him strength for every situation. He then expresses his profound gratitude to people all around the world who wrote to him while he was in prison. He kept careful count of all his letters: 67,985. He describes how they 'came in like a river every day' and reminded him of these words of :

> For this is what the LORD says:
> 'I will extend peace to her like a river,
> and the wealth of nations like a flooding stream . . .
> . . . As a mother comforts her child,
> so will I comfort you;
> and you will be comforted over Jerusalem.
> When you see this, your heart will rejoice . . .'
> (Isaiah 66:12–14, NIV)

He then gives two examples of ways in which different letters helped him. One was from a 14-year-old girl. She had enclosed a leaf, with these words: 'We may never know each other. But I believe you are my older brother. We are a poor family and I have nothing to send – except this leaf from our back yard.'

He said that he had always tried to smile and laugh all the time he was in prison. But when he saw that leaf, he cried: 'It was the only occasion I wept, during all my time in prison.' He went on to say that for a long time he could not understand the meaning of the leaf. Then he was greatly surprised – for the meaning came to him after his release, during his visit to Britain, when he believes God revealed it. He was reminded of Noah during the flood, in the ark on Mount Ararat, when he sent out a dove – and the dove returned with a leaf, symbolizing peace and new life outside the ark. The message was 'Soon you will be free and outside your ark.'

That letter came just before he was released – almost a year before the due date. The prayers and support of countless people around the world had been answered.

Another letter surprised him: it contained many pieces of sticking plaster, and in each piece of plaster he found that someone had written a Bible verse. There were 250 prisoners, of whom only five were Christians. As fighting amongst the men was not uncommon and prisoners were often injured, he used to give them his plasters. Although they were Muslims, they would read the verses from Scripture and would come to him to ask him to explain them. He describes how, in prison, there was a small chapel, so his Christian friends would take them there, open the Bible and show them the verse, hoping they would find comfort – and, possibly, Christ.

He comments, with a joyful smile: 'It was wonderful! Many came to believe in Christ because of those plasters. I believe those plasters were sent by people of faith and the Holy Spirit worked through them to touch the hearts of people in prison.'

Then his irrepressible sense of humour breaks out; he laughs, and says: 'Christ loves me so much! I don't know why! My faith tells me to believe in God and that God doesn't want me to work hard in prison, but to have a rest there! So some people send the Word of God on plasters; my friends help and I just sit back, relax and watch people open the Bible!'

He continues: 'I also really believe God left me in prison through his goodness, so that the Chief of Police and all the guards would know that Christians all over the world are united. One man with faith goes to prison for his faith and they are amazed by the thousands of letters he receives.'

Revd Damanik was released after serving two years and four months of his three-year sentence. Before his release, he was elected Chairperson of the Synod of Central and South

Sulawesi, with responsibility for 441 churches and 625 ministers.

But, at the time of writing, the situation in Sulawesi is very tense. On 29 October 2005 Islamic militants beheaded three Christian schoolgirls on their way home from school. The murdered girls were Theresia Murangke,14, Ida Lambuaga, 15, and Alfina Yarni Sambue, 15. At 7 a.m. on 29 October they were making their way to their Christian school through a cocoa plantation, a mile from the village of Sayo, near Poso city, Central Sulawesi. They were set upon by a group of men who attacked them with machetes. Half an hour later the three decapitated bodies were discovered. Later in the morning one head was found outside a church, eight miles from the scene of the attack (leading many to suspect a religious motive to the murders) and the other two heads were found near a police station five miles from Poso.

Letters were attached to the plastic bags in which the heads were found. The letters said that 100 more Christian teenagers would be slaughtered – and their heads would be given as gifts to Revd Damanik and other Christian leaders . . .

Chapter 3
Love like an ocean

One of the advantages of my work is that it allows me to visit some of the world's genuine heroes – people of exceptional courage and strength who risk their lives as followers of Christ and in the service of others. When I heard about the work of Sister Lourdes in East Timor, I took the first opportunity I could to visit her.

Just north of Australia, and on the tip of the Indonesian archipelago, East Timor was colonized by the Portuguese in the sixteenth century. Like Indonesia, it was occupied by the Japanese from 1942 to 1945, but Portugal then resumed its colonial rule. East Timor declared itself independent on 28 November 1975, but was invaded by Indonesia nine days later. In the two decades of fighting which followed, an estimated 100,000 to 250,000 people were killed; about 1,000,000 East Timorese remain. On 30 August 1999, in a referendum supervised by the United Nations, an overwhelming majority of the people of East Timor voted for independence. Indonesian-backed militias opposed to independence then launched a large-scale, scorched-earth campaign. Sister Lourdes was one of those who fought back with a message of love and reconciliation.

Sister Maria Lourdes (b. 1962), East Timor

'God worked a miracle,' says Sister Maria Lourdes. When fighting in East Timor was at its worst, 15,000 people left the city and found refuge in the forest around her house. 'We did not have enough food for even 15 people, let alone 15,000. But each day I got up, I prayed, and then I started cooking rice – and the barrel of rice never ran out for three weeks. The day it ran out was the day the international peacekeepers came.'

Stories of miracles abound in her ministry; her life itself is a miracle, because she has put herself in the face of danger numerous times, writes author and journalist Ben Rogers. During the violent occupation, many East Timorese priests and nuns courageously served their people despite the risks involved. But of all of them, it was Sister Lourdes who persistently went into the most dangerous areas where help was most urgently needed.

In April 1999, for example, in the period leading up to the referendum, a massacre occurred in the town of Liquica. People from nearby villages had fled the Indonesian-backed armed militia gangs who were terrorizing their areas, and sought refuge in Liquica parish church. They thought it would be a place of safety. Tragically, they were wrong. Indonesian military and their militia proxies threw tear gas into the church. As people ran out, the military opened fire, killing at random. A handful of people were hiding in the roof of the priest's house. When the Indonesians discovered this, they fired round after round into the ceiling, until the blood dripped through and they knew everyone up there was dead.

In the immediate aftermath of the massacre, Liquica was a scene of fear and confusion. Hundreds of people were displaced, having fled their homes. The militia did not kill them all, but kept the survivors captive. Trapped in the grounds of the church, under the watchful eyes of the militia, they were without food, medicine or shelter. Most of the village leaders had fled Liquica, but on their way out, they passed Sister Lourdes on her way in, driving through militia roadblocks with food and medicines. Miraculously, the militia allowed her to deliver aid to the captives, on the condition that any words she spoke should be restricted to spirituality, not politics.

According to Dr Daniel Murphy, an American doctor in East Timor, her ability to communicate was extraordinary. Faced with row after row of militia roadblocks, he recalls, she would get out of her car and speak to the militia. 'Within minutes she would have them laughing with her, then crying with her, and then on their knees praying with her.'

Sister Lourdes is crying as she talks to me about her life in East Timor. She tells me she was a young teenager when she realized her vocation: 'I desire to live for Christ; give my life for him. I think that human friends go away, but Christ stays with me and can make me a strong woman to help many other people.'

Leaving East Timor to study was her first major challenge: 'It was very hard to leave and study in Java with people who had killed my people. But I remembered God is my Father, so I wasn't going to Java alone. I was afraid of Muslim people and an Islamic country, but I felt I was with my family too, because of our heavenly Father.'

She stayed with a Muslim family and learned Indonesian so she could speak about the suffering of East Timor. 'Indonesian people believe East Timor people are primitive and uneducated. I told them how Indonesians came and burnt our homes; how we had to hide in the forest. But, I don't think they understood.'

While in Java, Sister Lourdes grappled with some difficult questions: 'I understand so little of what God wants. In Java I prayed so much for East Timor, speaking to God about colonialism. Why didn't he rescue us? He helped me think: if the Portuguese hadn't come to East Timor, we wouldn't know Christ and probably would have been Muslim. Many say Christianity isn't an East Timorese religion – but I want to take this Good News to my people.'

She adds, 'My time in Java was like an "engagement" with God, preparing for marriage.' She found herself talking to God, saying 'I love you; I want to do something for you.' Her growing love for the poor was an indication of her future vocation. She told me she loves beggars and wants to laugh with them and make them feel they are valued.

On her return to East Timor she was offered an official job, but refused it, not wanting to do what the government wanted. Instead she asked God what to do as she had no income. At 25 she could have opted for a successful career. Instead she began teaching in a religious school: 'I felt I must follow Christ's way.'

'They didn't pay anything,' she tells me. 'I worked 24 hours a week with no pay, but I was happy as I stayed in the village, organizing things for the children; they all loved me and gave me food.' Her father told her the bishop was probably testing her vocation by not paying her.

When a priest invited her to lead a retreat for young people she shared her vision of a simple life, travelling like Christ did. She told them, 'I want to live the Jesus life,' and she invited young people to stay with her to develop a mission for poor people. So her community – Maun Alin Iha Kristo (Brothers and Sisters of Christ) – began with sixteen girls.

At first the girls lived with their parents as Sister Lourdes had only one bed and no other furniture or facilities, but the girls' parents agreed to help by providing food and constructing a building. The first six months were very hard; sometimes the kitchen was empty, so they cooked papaya leaves, often laughing and crying together. Then a miracle happened. A Portuguese priest, with whom she had worked earlier, had a dream. In the dream he saw a community with no food on the table and people crying. He responded by sending money to Bishop Belo, the Bishop of Dili, to pay for a school building and food.

'I was asked to visit the bishop and thought perhaps he was going to give some money,' she recalls. He admitted that he hadn't wanted to help her, 'But now he knew we had started a work for God. God's work! "God has not left you alone, but is with you," he said.'

When the Bishop gave her the priest's letter she cried. 'The people around me had not understood my vision, but this priest had seen our situation in a dream. I discussed with the girls what we should do with the money. We bought food and filled a taxi with rice, then went to the chapel to sing and pray. After praying, we read the letter and realized how Christ had fulfilled his commitment to support us.'

Sister Lourdes has been heavily criticized for starting a community rather than joining an established order of nuns. 'But they [the girls] came with open minds and hearts,' she tells me. 'I explained that Christ is with us all and that they should not look at me, but should seek to experience him. They didn't look at the empty kitchen and run home to their parents; they trusted Christ. He called us for one mission together. He has repaid us.

'We minister to poor people and love and trust in God. If we only have material things, our life is empty. But our life is simple, blessed with love and fraternity. We don't see ourselves as poor but rich with people and the capacity to transform our lives, and those of others, with our riches.'

Sister Lourdes admits she often feels tired and alone: 'I cry so much. I look at the cross and feel God saying: "You don't feel my presence; I'm in your heart always. You say you are alone; you don't recognize my presence. I don't want you to continue to live this way, lamenting alone. You have my presence always. You have classrooms and people: make them love me and know me; transform them; change their lives. There are many clever people, but you must change the world. Therefore, pray for the Holy Spirit and remember you are not alone. Do not cry. Don't worry about problems. Make your girls strong and don't let them see you are tired."'

Sister Lourdes' community has set up a health education programme and a 'sick house', recognized by the Government's Social Department. As news of her work spread, one NGO asked her to send a proposal for funding. But then they rejected it, saying it was 'very spiritual'.

They then asked her to resubmit the proposal and sent their secretary to help, but he wanted them to change everything, including their vision and principles. They had an interest in women's groups and wanted Sister Lourdes to fit their funding criteria.

'They offered a large amount of money but it wasn't for spiritual things,' she tells me. 'I felt I had become a slave to money, so I replied: "I'm sorry, but I must protect what God wants for poor people. I must follow what God wants, not what money wants."'

The NGO replied, 'You always speak about what God wants . . . My organization isn't a religious organization. Don't come to me for help.'

People thought she was crazy for refusing to apply for the money. 'This made me very ashamed,' she says. 'My girls were very nervous, so I went to the chapel and prayed.'

She returned with fresh energy and determination and told the charity's secretary: 'I don't want to go to "rich people" because they don't understand me. I work for "poor people" with "poor people".'

With that, she turned to go home, but the man followed her, asking for her building proposal. Apparently 'the Boss' was waiting. Miraculously, the charity had a change of heart. Sister Lourdes says, 'When I returned the Boss embraced me, saying, "I feel ashamed. I'm a man, with three children, and you are a woman on your own, thinking so much about poor people. What can I do for you?"

'I showed him my proposal and he sent a big truck with everything we needed for our building – and he came to advise us. I explained our vision for the poor and I said, "Praise the Lord that you understand God's vision." We were so happy. We had our building and a roof just before the rainy season – and we had learned to trust God.'

Sister Lourdes has not sought fame or reward. She is resolute in her commitment to follow Christ without compromise. When she was honoured with the international Pax Christi Peace Award, she says, 'I wasn't interested, because my prize is in heaven. I didn't ask for money, but hid in the mountains and people came with money.' Groups in East Timor asked her to join them, 'but I didn't want to mix my life with politics, so I stayed here.'

With tension mounting throughout the country in 1999, Sister Lourdes says, 'I prayed and said to God, "Now the suffering has started; you prepared us for this. What do you want us to do?"'

She spoke boldly to a general's wife, who had become a friend; to the civilian authorities; and to the Muslim military authorities, often quoting the street preacher and prophet Ezekiel – she could see parallels between this biblical character's circumstances and her situation in contemporary East Timor. Rather than rejecting what she had to say, the mayor of

Liquica invited her to speak about the parallels and to lead a retreat preparing people for the referendum.

'I taught the children songs about the bad things the military had done,' she tells me. 'Then we held hands, even with those who had killed the people in the church. We tried to show our love to them, to pray for them, to stop any more killing.

'There was a military leader who had killed many people. His daughter was ill, so we prayed for guidance. The girls then stood with candles and I spoke to the man, asking him to leave his job, believing God had another plan for him. If he converted and changed his ways, his daughter could possibly recover. The girls and everyone present asked him to repeat the prayer: "Jesus forgive me, for I have killed many people."'

He did; his daughter asked for a drink, then began to recover.

'That night, the man came and said: "I will leave and not kill any more. I only did so under pressure from the Indonesian Army – but I will not kill again."'

In August 1999, the referendum on independence was finally held, despite the tense atmosphere. Over 90 per cent of the electorate turned out at the polling stations, braving the militias' threats and intimidation. Almost 80 per cent of them voted for independence.

The East Timorese won their long-sought independence, and a three-year transition period under United Nations administration began. But they paid a high price for independence. Within hours of the referendum, East Timor was plunged into yet more terror. In the weeks it took the United Nations to decide how to respond, thousands died, and hundreds of thousands were displaced, at the hands of pro-Indonesian militias. Finally, an Australian-led peacekeeping force entered East Timor and restored order.

During the worst violence immediately following the referendum, an estimated 15,000 people fled the capital, Dili, and sought refuge in the forest around Sister Lourdes' house, set in her father's coffee plantation in the mountains above Dare. That was when the miracle happened. As the terrified men, women and children fled into hiding in the jungle around

Sister Lourdes' community, the sisters started to cook rice for them. As more people came, they continued to cook rice. Eventually, they were cooking rice for 15,000 people, and the container – which normally held only enough for the small community's daily needs – never became empty, until the day the international peacekeepers arrived and it was safe for the people to return to their homes. Only then did the rice cooker return to its normal behaviour!

Even after the United Nations arrived in East Timor, Sister Lourdes' work with the militia and the refugees was not complete. Thousands of East Timorese were still being held by militia in camps in Indonesian-held West Timor and so, in the spring of 2001, Sister Lourdes went there to try to persuade refugees to return home, and to help meet their basic physical needs and give them spiritual support.

The camps were still controlled by militia who, she said, wanted to kill her. Each time Sister Lourdes held a meeting with refugees to speak to them about the situation in East Timor and persuade them to return, bare-chested, menacing militia would ride their motorbikes right into the meeting. Sitting inches from her, they would rev their engines, attempting to intimidate her. She decided to confront the militiamen, but not with fear, anger, or hatred. She confronted them with faith.

'Will you come home?' she asked them. 'Will you come home to the Father's house – to God?' As she spoke with them, many of these militiamen – thugs who were guilty of horrific crimes – broke down in tears and converted to Christianity. Those who converted then joined her in her work of encouraging the refugees to return home – the very refugees these militiamen had been holding hostage.

Chapter 4

Mystery – not misery

During many visits to the borderlands between Burma and Thailand, as well as when crossing unofficially into Burma, I have encountered very many people from the Karen, Karenni, Shan, Chin and Kachin ethnic groups. I have listened to their accounts of the atrocities perpetrated against them by the brutal regime which holds power in Burma today. Civilians are used as human minesweepers, forced to walk ahead of soldiers. Children tell me they have seen their brothers and sisters ground to death in a log-weighted rice pounder. Elderly people are forced to carry heavy loads of rice and ammunition from dawn until dusk; they are beaten, kicked and sometimes left for dead if they fail to carry out the soldiers' orders. Families are forced to hide in the jungle and scavenge for their existence. People lack the basic necessities of food and medicine; on one visit we came to a village in which a schoolteacher ran to us saying that his food supplies were exhausted and he had nothing to give the children; on my last visit I met a mother whose five children had just died from malaria. My colleague, Dr Martin Panter, has examined people vomiting blood, their skin blistering because of chemical weapons attacks. Thriving communities with churches, schools, houses and clinics have been turned to ashes in the fierce fighting, as Karen, Karenni, Shan, Chin and Kachin struggle for freedom from oppression at the hands of a brutal Burmese regime.

Nobel laureate Aung San Suu Kyi's peaceful resistance to oppression in Burma has meant many years of prison and house arrest – but it has brought Burma (also known as Myanmar – a name which is intensely disliked by the local people whom we meet) to the attention of the world. In 1990 the Burmese people elected her party, the National League for Democracy, by an 80 per cent majority. It was doomed to political annihilation when the present regime, the Orwellian-sounding State Peace and Development Council, seized power by force. Even though Aung San Suu Kyi is under house arrest, her voice is still heard. Less so are the voices of the country's national ethnic groups, who are dying in their thousands under the military dictatorship's policy of cultural and physical genocide.

Pastor Simon (b. 1949), Burma

It was in this context of horrific human rights abuses that I first met Pastor Simon. This powerful meditation of his, which he gave to me personally during one of my visits, sums up his attitude to life in this zone of suffering:

> They call us a displaced people,
> But praise God; we are not misplaced.
> They say they see no hope for our future,
> But praise God; our future is as bright as the
>   promises of God.
> They say they see the life of our people is a misery,
> But praise God; our life is a mystery.
> For what they say is what they see,
> And what they see is temporal.
> But ours is the eternal.
> All because we put ourselves
> In the hands of the God we trust.

To anyone else, Pastor Simon's circumstances are bleak, but he has transformed the deprivations of life in a camp for the displaced, from a situation of despair into a place of hope. He has established a theological seminary in the camp and cares for many Karen children, including orphans who have had to flee from their homes in Burma in order to survive.

He returned to his Karen people in Burma after studying in the Philippines. As he had a seminary education, he was elected as president of the school in Wallai in South Karen

State. At the end of 1989, the school was attacked by the ruling military junta, which was then called SLORC (the State Law and Order Restoration Council), so Pastor Simon had to flee across the border to Mae La Camp in Thailand. He became the president of a school with no building, teachers or students, so he prayed and invited teachers to Mae La and he spoke with the camp leadership and pastors. Eventually they were able to open a school in 1990. In the original school in Wallai, there had been only 43 students; now, in Mae La, there are 333.

He told me 1996 was a particularly difficult year. Towards the end of 1995 the Karen Army split apart with the formation of the DKBA (Democratic Karen Buddhist Army) – a splinter movement supported by the regime in Burma. The Karen HQ at Manerplaw fell in early 1996 and the three camps across the border in Thailand were attacked. The other two camps were destroyed. At Mae La, where they had gone for safety, two women and some students were killed and sixteen houses burnt. Pastor Simon recalls, 'When the army approached, everyone ran, people were screaming, children crying; no-one knew where to run.'

Pastor Simon called his family and teachers together. The security forces asked them to move to a safer place, so Pastor Simon asked his wife, daughters and volunteer teachers to go. But he remained at the school.

'I stayed with some students and we prayed for God's power. He answered; I felt a burning sensation, with no fear. I felt that if DKBA came to kill us it would be all right, but I would ask them to allow me to preach to them first. I would explain their name and what it means:

D stands for democracy and freedom.

K for Karen – so why, as Karen, were they killing their own people?

B for Buddhist. I grew up in a Buddhist country and studied Buddhist teachings about good works and goodness; the four noble truths and the eightfold path.

A for army. They are soldiers and should fight the enemy, not unarmed civilians. Why attack them?

'I thought, if they kill me it will be all right, so long as I can preach to them. Then I realized they would already be drugged and drunk, so it would be no good trying to teach them – the soldiers are always drugged before being sent to fight.

'Then another thought occurred to me: although they are bad people, they are created by God and He loves them and can help them. So I prayed: "Dear God, those who attack us are your children and you have power over them. Give them fear so they will run away and not attack our people."

'Immediately, the shooting stopped. There had been intense shooting, but suddenly all went quiet. We heard later they had suddenly become afraid, dropped their weapons, leaving them behind, and fled.

'After a few days, they attacked again. This time, they didn't come but shelled the camp and shot from across the border in Burma. The people were terrified. So I called the teachers and students at midnight to come to pray.

'Some Thai soldiers were curious and also came. We explained we did not want this fighting. When shooting from across the border began again, they were targeting us and a rocket hit part of the camp. We prayed to God for a miracle to stop the firing. Then we heard, from the Thai side, that a monster shell had exploded; immediately the shooting stopped and everything became quiet. The shell had hit their gun emplacement direct and there was no more shooting.'

Pastor Simon has experienced many miracles of God's protection and provision. On other occasions, situations which had seemed disastrous brought surprise blessings.

'On 24 September 1996 there was a huge flood, the greatest we had ever known,' he says. 'It destroyed our church and our kitchen. This created great difficulties, but the hardship became a blessing in disguise. We wrote letters asking for help and Australian Baptists sent money for us to build a new church and a new kitchen. Now we have a bigger church than the one we had before.'

Even though Pastor Simon was living in the camp in the jungle, he wanted to complete his Ph.D. thesis in order to enhance his ministry. However, he thought he needed to carry

27

out the final stage in his own country – Burma – since the initial stages of his thesis research had involved questionnaires and interviews which had to be followed up. But, since the seizure of power by the new regime, all the questionnaires and interviews he had prepared were useless. Also, his original supervisor had died, so he wrote to the Asian Baptist Graduate Theological Seminary (ABGTS). The dean went to visit him although he was partly paralysed and couldn't walk properly. It was the rainy season and it had been raining heavily. Pastor Simon met him at the airport and took him to a hotel, but he wanted to visit the camp. The road was so bad that Pastor Simon had to carry the dean on his back for the last part of the way. After a few hours, he took him back the same way. The dean was so touched that he wept, and he agreed that Pastor Simon could continue the dissertation with a new supervisor and a slight modification to allow him to complete his own work while in exile.

When Pastor Simon was invited to the Philippines for the awarding of his doctorate, it was not possible for him to travel, because Thailand would not allow him to return. So the ABGTS sent a delegation to Thailand to confer the degree in Chiang Mai. But Pastor Simon couldn't even go to Chiang Mai, so the dignitaries came to the camp and conferred the degree in the church, where all the church members and the Thai officers could witness the ceremony – 'another miracle!' says Pastor Simon.

In 2000, the Baptist World Alliance announced that they had awarded Pastor Simon their Human Rights Award - only the second one to be given: the first was given to Jimmy Carter in 1995. Pastor Simon was greatly surprised, thinking he was 'only a little guy'. Once again, he couldn't travel abroad, for fear of being refused re-entry to Thailand. As he was unable to go to Melbourne to receive the award, the Baptist World Alliance sent a delegation to Chiang Mai. However serious fighting meant he couldn't go there to receive it, so, once again the award ceremony took place in the church.

Even in the details of these award ceremonies, God seems to

have honoured Pastor Simon's commitment to stay with his church, turning his deprivations into blessings for his people.

I am pleased that former president of the Czech Republic Vaclav Havel, together with Nobel Peace Prize laureate and Archbishop Emeritus of Cape Town, Desmond Tutu, have added their voices to calls for change in Burma. In September 2005, they commissioned a report calling for a new, multilateral diplomatic initiative at the UN Security Council to prompt change in Burma.

Bishop Tutu first became known as the voice of resistance to the apartheid government in South Africa. His book *God has a Dream*, published in 2004, shares the spiritual values that guided him and gave him hope in those troubled times; values and insights which can give hope to others around the world facing similar, seemingly hopeless situations:

> During the darkest days of apartheid I used to say to P. W. Botha, the president of South Africa, that we had already won, and I invited him and other white South Africans to join the winning side. All the 'objective' facts were against us – the pass laws, the imprisonments, the tear-gassing, the massacres, the murder of political activists – but my confidence was not in the present circumstances but in the laws of God's universe. This is a *moral* universe, which means that, despite all the evidence that seems to be to the contrary, there is no way that evil and injustice and oppression and lies can have the last word. God is a God who cares about right and wrong. God cares about justice and injustice. God is in charge. That is what had upheld the morale of our people, to know that in the end good will prevail. It was these higher laws that convinced me that our peaceful struggle would topple the immoral laws of apartheid.
>
> Of course, there were times when you had to whistle in the dark to keep your morale up, and you wanted to whisper in God's ear: 'God, we know You are in charge, but can't You make it a little more obvious?'[1]

Asia

When apartheid was in full swing, God did make that fact more obvious. Tutu and other church leaders were preparing for a meeting with the prime minister. During the discussions Tutu went into a priory garden for some quiet. A large wooden cross caught his attention.

It was a stark symbol of the Christian faith . . . As I sat quietly in the garden I realized the power of transfiguration – of God's transformation – in our world. The principle of transfiguration is at work when something so unlikely as the brown grass that covers our veld in winter becomes bright green again . . . Christian history is filled with examples of transfiguration . . . I doubt, however, that we could produce a more spectacular example of this principle of transfiguration than the Cross itself. Most people would have been filled with revulsion had someone gone and set up an electric chair or a gallows or the guillotine as an object of reverence. Well, look at the Cross. It was a ghastly instrument of death, of an excruciatingly awful death reserved for the most notorious malefactors. It was an object of dread and shame, and yet what a turnaround has happened. This instrument of a horrendous death has been spectacularly transfigured. Once a means of death, it is now perceived by Christians to be the source of life eternal. Far from being an object of vilification and shame, it is an object of veneration.[2]

Chapter 5

Paying the ultimate price

The Western media rarely report news of Christians facing false accusations, imprisonment and death because of their faith – but these things happen regularly. Here are just a few of the tragic events in Asia reported by human rights groups during the last few years.

Severino Bagtasos (d. January 1996), Philippines

On a Sunday morning in January 1996, Severino Bagtasos was killed when a lone gunman stormed into the church, which he served as pastor, in the predominantly Muslim town of Alat on Jolo island, in the south Philippines. The gunman shot him twice and he died instantly.

Open Doors reported that Severino was killed on the first day of the Islamic holy month of Ramadan. Some Muslim sects believe that if you kill an enemy of Allah on the first day of Ramadan, the act will ensure your passage into Paradise. This belief, plus Severino's zeal in teaching Muslims about Christ, fuelled his killer's desire to murder him.

Ayub Masih (sentenced to death, 1998), Pakistan

Ayub Masih was sentenced to death in 1998, having been falsely accused of blasphemy against Muhammad. Assist News reports that it was an allegation Ayub always denied – arguing that the accusation followed an attempt by his Muslim landlord to evict him from his home. Ayub Masih only avoided execution when the Supreme Court of Pakistan finally upheld his

Asia

appeal and, in August 2002, quashed the charges against him. Writing in *Just Right* magazine, Ayub Masih says, 'I was miraculously delivered from the death penalty, confinement in prison and a fine of 100,000 rupees [about US$1,800]. I could not believe that I would see the light of day once again. During these days, the extremists announced a reward for anyone who succeeded in killing me and I was attacked and stabbed in prison by four Muslim inmates. That is why I am grateful for the help I received from the Jubilee Campaign to flee Pakistan and to establish a new life in a new country.'[1]

Graham, Philip and Timothy Staines (d. January 1999), India

Graham Staines, who ran a leprosy home at Baripada in Mayurbhanj district, and his two sons Philip, eleven, and Timothy, eight, were asleep in their estate car at Manoharpur village in Keonjhar district on the night of 22 January 1999 when a crowd surrounded them and set the vehicle ablaze, killing all three.

I had the great privilege of meeting Graham's wife Gladys not long after the murder of her husband and two sons. I will never forget her lack of bitterness and the way in which she spoke of forgiveness. She was a very powerful witness to the power of Christ's transforming grace, which can turn brutality and hatred into love and forgiveness.

Ranjha Masih (life sentence, April 2003), Pakistan

On Saturday 26 April 2003, Ranjha Masih, 55, was sentenced to life imprisonment with a fine of 50,000 rupees (approximately US$900) for allegedly committing blasphemy.

On 8 May 1998, Ranjha Masih was part of a large crowd mourning the death of his long-time personal friend, the

Bishop of Faislabad, Dr John Joseph, who had shot himself in the head outside the Faislabad courthouse on 6 May 1998 in protest against the blasphemy law – in particular the judgement of the district and session judge of Sahiwal Court, who had imposed the death penalty on Ayub Masih.

The prosecution accused Masih of participating in a 'violent Christian procession' and smashing a neon sign bearing the Muslim statement of faith.

Ranjha Masih was arrested on 8 May 1998 and was held in prison without bail for the five years prior to his trial. According to Assist News, the Christian Liberation Front (CLF) has been closely monitoring his case. In December 2002, when CLF president Shabhaz Bhatti personally met Ranjha Masih in Faisalbad Central Jail, Masih said: 'I will be happy if the sacrifice of my life could contribute in the abolishment of this black law of blasphemy, although I am falsely involved and being punished for a crime that I did not commit. The prayers of my brothers and sisters in Christ are strength for me.'

Dulal Sarkar (d. March 2004), Bangladesh

Dulal Sarkar, 35, worked with a local branch of the Bangladesh Free Baptist Church in Jalalpur village, in the southwest division of Khulna, Compass Direct reports. He had planted several churches in the area and also worked as a guard and general caretaker for the church.

The week before he was murdered, he shared his faith with several Muslim villagers who became Christians. He then brought them to the church for counselling with the senior pastor.

On 8 March 2004 Sarkar once again spoke about his faith with a number of villagers. On his way home, he was attacked by a group of armed men who, as one source said, 'separated his head from his body'. The assailants were later identified as a group of ten local Muslim extremists.

Assad Ullah (d. June 2004), Naveed ul-Rehman (d. August 2004) and others (d. July 2004), Afghanistan

Five Afghan men who had converted to Christianity were killed in separate incidents between June and September 2004 near the borders of eastern Afghanistan, according to Compass Direct. All five men were stabbed or beaten to death in summary executions by Taliban adherents who accused them of abandoning Islam and then 'spreading Christianity' in their communities.

The first stabbing death was reported on 1 July by Reuters news agency, which received a telephone call from a Taliban spokesman identifying himself as Abdul Latif Hakimi. The caller declared that a group of Taliban fighters had killed Mullah Assad Ullah the previous day in Ghazni province's remote Awdand region, a known Taliban stronghold and traditional seat of Islamic learning.

'A group of Taliban dragged out Mullah Assad Ullah and slit his throat with a knife because he was propagating Christianity,' Hakimi told Reuters. 'We have enough evidence and local accounts to prove that he was involved in the conversion of Muslims to Christianity.'

Hakimi went on to accuse a number of foreign aid agencies of involvement in spreading Christianity among Afghanistan's overwhelmingly Muslim population. 'We warn them that they face the same destiny as Assad Ullah if they continue to seduce people,' he told Reuters. At least 33 foreign aid workers have been killed by the Taliban in the past eighteen months.

According to local sources, Assad Ullah was seized in broad daylight while at the market buying fruit and vegetables for his family. His attackers reportedly dragged his dead body around the market area, shouting warnings that the same fate awaited anyone else who listened to his teachings.

The former mullah had first obtained a copy of the New Testament about five years previously, while still living under the Taliban regime. He had been baptized secretly. In his mid-forties, Assad Ullah is survived by a widow and four daughters, ages seven to fourteen.

The murder of another Afghan convert to Christianity who had gone to visit Assad Ullah's family was confirmed on 7 August. According to a fellow convert, the body of Naveed ul-Rehman was discovered in early August near his abandoned car in Awdand, at the same marketplace where the former mullah had been killed. Nothing had been stolen from ul-Rehman's pockets or car, nor was any evidence found to reveal the identity of his attackers. About 40 years old, ul-Rehman was a well-educated Afghan who had been living in Kabul since his return to Afghanistan. He was married without children.

During the month of July 2005 another three Afghan Christians were stabbed or beaten to death in separate incidents on 15 July, 23 July and 28 July. Each left behind a wife and several children. The three men had been accused by their attackers of studying the Bible, praying in the name of Jesus or associating with other known Afghan converts to Christianity.

Abdul Gani (d. September 2004), Bangladesh

On 18 September 2004, Dr Abdul Gani, a prominent Christian in Bangladesh, was decapitated by a gang of assailants as he returned home from work around 9:30 p.m.

A Compass Direct source close to the doctor reported, 'The moment he came under a banyan tree, these terrorist people attacked him and slaughtered him with sharp knives. We Christians are all very sad about this event.'

Dr Abdul Gani and his family converted to Christianity in 1995. He was a respected Christian leader and medical practitioner in his home district of Jamalpur, 140 kilometres north of Dhaka.

Abdul Gani – also known by his Christian name, Joseph Gomez – was a member of the Bangladesh Baptist Fellowship council and frequently worked with members of the Catholic Church.

According to an Asia News report, he once mortgaged his own home to raise funds for flood victims. Neighbours described him as a very compassionate man.

Tapan Kumar Roy and Liplal Marandi (d. July 2005), Bangladesh

Two Christian health workers in Bangladesh were hacked to death on 29 July 2005, Compass Direct reports. Police and local officials believe Islamic extremists were probably responsible for the murders. The incident took place about 150 kilometres from the capital, Dhaka.

Tapan Kumar Roy, 30, and Liplal Marandi, 35, worked for Christian Life Bangladesh (CLB). Along with educational films on arsenic poisoning, mother-and-child health care and AIDS prevention, they often showed the film *Jesus*, a two-hour docudrama of the life of Christ based on the Gospel of Luke, at the invitation of local villagers.

A well-known Christian leader familiar with the two evangelists said an official at a local *madrassa* (Islamic school) had threatened the men verbally prior to the murders. Some villagers had also threatened to kill Roy and Marandi if they continued to show *Jesus*.

Feroz Masih (attacked and beaten, November 2005), India

Hindu extremists attacked 62-year-old pastor Feroz Masih in the north Indian state of Himachal Pradesh on 4 November 2005, accusing him of 'forcibly converting' Hindus and beating him severely. In November 2005 Compass Direct reported: 'The attackers then forced Masih to sign a document saying he was willing to participate in a ceremony in which all 60 members of his church would be converted back to Hinduism. If the pastor and other church members refused to take part, the extremists threatened to burn them to death.' The planned reconversion ceremony was apparently dropped due to police intervention.

Communist Asia   II

Chapter 1

Faithful unto death

We patiently endure troubles and hardships and calamities of every kind. We have been beaten, been put in jail, faced angry mobs, worked to exhaustion, endured sleepless nights, and gone without food. We have proved ourselves by our purity, our understanding, our patience, our kindness, our sincere love, and the power of the Holy Spirit. We have faithfully preached the truth. God's power has been working in us. We have righteousness as our weapon, both to attack and to defend ourselves. We serve God whether people honour us or despise us, whether they slander us or praise us. We are honest, but they call us impostors. We are well known, but we are treated as unknown. We live close to death, but here we are, still alive. We have been beaten within an inch of our lives. Our hearts ache, but we always have joy. We are poor, but we give spiritual riches to others. We own nothing, and yet we have everything.

These could be the words of Christians living under persecution in Indonesia; equally, they could be spoken by Christians in Asia's communist countries: China, North Korea, Vietnam and Laos. They are in fact the words of the Apostle Paul to the Corinthian church (2 Corinthians 6:4–10, New Living Translation), which echo through two thousand years of persecution faced by Christians since then.

The People's Republic of China was established in 1949 when the Communist Party came to power under Mao Zedong. Foreign missionaries were forced to leave and during the next thirty years the Chinese church was forced 'underground', churches were closed and church leaders were persecuted. Samuel Lamb, Allen Yuan, Wang Ming Dao, and Watchman Nee are four examples of Chinese church leaders who spent many years in prison for their faith.

I visited China in the 1980s with a group of nurses from Hong Kong. We went to Guangzhou to introduce the concept, philosophy and practices of palliative care for the terminally ill, which had been pioneered in Britain by Dame Cicely Saunders and her colleagues in the hospice movement. In one of the hospitals specializing in the care of patients with cancer, we met the Chinese nurses and discussed ways in which this approach to the care of the dying and their families could be applied in the context of Chinese culture – as well as in the busy, overcrowded hospitals in Guangzhou. As the next day was Sunday, my nursing friends asked me if I would like to worship with them at Pastor Lamb's house church. Having heard so much about this man who had suffered so much for his faith, I eagerly agreed.

We had to arrive an hour early to gain access to the main floor where he would be leading the communion service. We climbed the stairs of this small, humble house and sat in pews so tightly packed that it was impossible to cross one's knees. Quickly, people poured into the small room, many kneeling before the simple altar, in devout prayer. Before the service was due to start, the entire house had filled with people crammed into every available inch to hear the service relayed to each floor.

The simplicity and sincerity of the worship was beautiful. Pastor Lamb preached passionately – and, for a wimpish Westerner unused to sitting cramped in one position for nearly three hours, it seemed long! But the congregation was lost in rapt attention. At the end of the service, Pastor Lamb graciously welcomed the foreign guests, apologizing for a sore throat, which meant he could not preach for as long as usual. Some of us could not resist the unworthy thought that we were not too sorry to have picked that particular day! But that very thought reminded us of how much we who live in the West, with our 'comfortable Christianity', take for granted. Perhaps we miss the depth of spirituality which can transcend minor discomfort in the experience of a joy which this world can neither give nor take away. Indeed, whenever I have the opportunity to worship with churches suffering persecution, I am always humbled beyond words by the radiance and joy of their worship – having nothing, yet having all things.

Samuel Lamb (b. 1924), Guangzhou, China

Samuel Lamb celebrated his eightieth birthday on 4 October 2004. A quarter of his life has been spent in prison for his faith. He still preaches several times on Sunday in his large house church and most weeknights in Bible studies, reports Open Doors. His brilliant smile shines from a slight body suffering chronic disability resulting from fifteen years' confinement in a coal mine. 'God gives me the strength I need,' he says. He has never left China, fearing that if he travelled, the authorities would not let him return.

Lamb credits God for the faith to accept what has happened in his life. It has deepened his ministry. Lamb believes that sometimes God is more glorified through sickness and poverty than through health and wealth. Christians travel thousands of miles to discuss house church ministry with Pastor Lamb and visitors from around the world seek out his church in Guangzhou, China, which gathers 3,000 members each week. Lamb often refers to persecution and growth as intertwined. He is known for his quotation, 'Remember the lesson of the Chinese church: more persecution, more growth.' As the pastor explains, 'Before I was put into prison in 1955, this church's membership was 400; when I came out in 1978, it built up to 900 in a matter of weeks. Then after 1990, when everything was confiscated here and the church briefly closed, we re-opened and in a matter of weeks we had 2,000 members. More persecution, more growth – that's the history of the Chinese church, that's the history of this church.'

Born of Christian parents in 1924 in Macau, his Chinese name, Lin Xiangao, means 'to offer to the Lamb of God'. His family's surname was Lam, so with his birth name and his Christian name, he was clearly marked for service to the body of Christ. In 1938, his father gave him the name Samuel.

Lamb's talents and faith grew under persecution. On a whim, he began cutting hair in his school days, and his skills as a barber provided many opportunities for him to minister one-on-one while he was in prison. He loves music and trained as a concert pianist. His practice on the church piano led to him preaching his first sermon. He wrote many hymns in prison which are sung by the Chinese church today.

He also memorized large portions of the New Testament and Psalms when the Japanese invasion of World War II kept him isolated in Hong Kong. These verses fed his soul during his many years of imprisonment.

Marrying when he was 25, Lamb and his wife Sing Yin had three children. Their first son died when he was just 33 hours old. A daughter, Hannah, and son, Enoch, were born in the next few years.

Lamb's first imprisonment, of nearly 18 months, occurred in 1955. To make ends meet when he returned home from prison, his wife returned to nursing in her father's medical practice, only seeing Samuel and little Enoch at weekends. Their daughter Hannah was raised by another relative. When Samuel was arrested a second time in late summer 1958, he saw his wife only briefly for short prison visits in the five months before his court sentencing. She died just a year before he returned, after serving that final twenty-year sentence for his faith. Their life together was short.

Lamb's own faith grew through several incidents when the Lord seemed miraculously to have preserved his life. When he was five years old, the all-night prayers of church members were believed to have brought him out of an extremely critical case of diphtheria. During World War II, he recalls changing the route of his daily walk only to see a bomb explode in the spot where he would have been.

The same hand was at work while Lamb was imprisoned. During his fifteen years in a coal mine, a loaded coal car careered down the track toward him. At the moment of certain death, he felt wrapped in glowing peace. He thought of God's promise: 'He shall give his angels charge over thee, to keep thee in all thy ways.' As if restrained by the mighty arm of an angel, the car stopped, pinning Lamb firmly but unharmed to the wall of the mine.

Finally discharged after twenty years, Lamb went unrecognized when he stepped off the bus on 17 July 1978, in his home town of Guangzhou. The door to his home at 35 Da Ma Zhan was locked, but another entrance led to the upper floor. The Red Guards had ransacked the Lamb residence, taking all the Bibles and literature, and confiscating the property, but leaving them with the second level.

A quiet invitation to conduct services at a home on 25 March 1979 led to a church being started. Lamb resumed services at 35 Da Ma Zhan in September 1979, and attendance climbed quickly from four or five people to an average of over 300 believers at each Sunday service.

On 19 November 1988, the *Washington Post* ran a three-column article about the house church ministry at 35 Da Ma Zhan, along with a photograph of Samuel Lamb. The article claimed that from late 1983 through 1986, Lamb's house church congregation grew to 'some 1,300 followers living in and around Guangzhou'.

More visitors began coming to the meetings. Greetings and gifts were sent by then President Reagan and Vice-President George Bush. Dr and Mrs Billy Graham came to a service; and astronaut James Irwin also visited.

From August to December 1988, the Public Security Bureau (PSB) summoned Lamb for questioning six times. They asked him to register officially with the Three Self Patriotic Movement (TSPM), the official, government-controlled church in China, but he refused. Then on 22 February 1990, over sixty PSB officers detained him overnight and confiscated large amounts of Christian literature from his house church. China's best-known Protestant pastor was left in relative peace after this, although police called him in for questioning and confiscated 2,500 Bibles on 6 November 1995, and again questioned him on 29 August 1998.

More recently, on Sunday, 13 June 2004, Chinese authorities detained and interrogated him after worship services, along with ten of his younger co-workers. Taken to a local police station in Guangzhou, all were released by the following day.

Allen Yuan (1914–2005), China

'The church is a virgin bride prepared for the coming Bride-groom, not a whore to work for the government'. That was the blunt statement which landed Allen Yuan in prison. He, like Pastor Lamb, was among the church leaders who refused to join the TSPM.

Yuan received a life sentence, leaving his mother, his wife and six children, aged six to seventeen, without support. He was released in December 1979, having served a total of 21 years and eight months. In his testimony, published by Voice of the Martyrs, he wrote,

> During those years in prison my wife suffered untold hardships in bringing up the children. I was sent to near the Russian border doing farm work, growing rice. Wang Ming Dao and I thought we would die martyrs there.
>
> In the labour camp it was very cold, food was bad, and the work was hard, but in 22 years I never once got sick. I was thin and wore glasses, but I came back alive; many did not. I also had no Bible for the 22 years and there were no other Protestant Christians there. I met only four Catholic priests. They were in the same situation I was in; they refused to join the Chinese Catholic Patriotic Association.[1]

Yuan was born in 1914 in South China, and his family moved to Beijing in 1928. Initially he dismissed Christianity as a Western religion, but after examining Buddhism and Confucianism, he became a Christian. He studied at the Far East Theological Seminary and by 1946 he was back in Beijing where he started a church in a rented hall; every year between twenty and fifty people were baptized and joined the church.

In 1950, a year after the Communist takeover, the government set up the Three Self Patriotic Movement to develop Chinese churches under government control. Yuan and other pastors, including Wang Ming Dao and Watchman Nee, refused to join. Yuan was arrested in 1958 and sentenced to life in prison.

After his release, Yuan returned to lead a growing church. In 1998, when he baptized more than three hundred new Christians, he was placed under house arrest. However, he continued to lead an unregistered house church, baptizing about three hundred new converts each year in a nondescript area outside of Beijing.

Allen Yuan died in a Beijing hospital on 16 August 2005, surrounded by his wife and six children. He was 91. One of his sons continues to lead the church, which was reported to have baptized more than seven hundred people in the year before Yuan died.

Wang Ming Dao (1900–1991), China

An outspoken critic of the government and its official church, Wang Ming Dao was sent to prison in 1955 for 'resistance to the government' – refusing to join the Three Self Patriotic Movement. After some time in prison he succumbed to intense pressure; his faith wavered, he signed a 'confession' and was released. However, he subsequently deeply regretted his capitulation and told the authorities that the confession, signed under duress, did not express his true feelings. As a result he was returned to prison in 1958 to face a twenty-year sentence.

He was released in 1980 after spending twenty-three years in prison. In 1989, he was asked: 'Do you have a message for the outside world?' He replied: 'Tell them to walk the hard road.' It was a message he put into practice. He explained:

> In my long life I have known all kinds of trials and testings. Psalm 66 really describes all that I have been through. Verse 12 says, 'We have passed through the waters and through the fire, but you cause us to come to a place of great abundance.'
>
> I have been through fire and water. The water was deep and the fire blazing. But all these have passed away. Many times in the last 20 years I have come close to death. But each time I have passed safely through . . . All these things have been entirely to my good.

I have suffered many serious illnesses. In 1961 through 1962 I was desperately ill, lying flat out on my bed for a whole year, spitting blood. Would I have said at that time that I was going to live? But God performed a miracle. After an entire year, He healed me completely. Two years or so after that, I had an X-ray taken which showed that there was no trace of disease and that the damaged portions of the lung were already renewed.

After that came many other trials and evils – things that are not easy for tongue to describe. But thanks be to God, He has caused my faith (apart from that one point where I wavered) to stand firm to the end . . . As a matter of fact, He has strengthened that faith so that it is firmer now than it was before.

From this, I can now understand that God's way of working within the lives of those whom He loves is truly wonderful. The experiences I remember best are those that revealed God's presence. His power. His wisdom and His grace . . .

To summarize it all is to say simply that God has allowed me to go through many trials and adversities, all of them to test and refine me. He has done this so that in the end I might be stronger than ever, more pure-hearted, more loyal toward my God.

I remember the words of Jesus to his church as recorded in Revelation 2:10 (King James Version), 'Fear none of those things which thou shalt suffer: behold, the devil shall cast some of you into prison, that ye may be tried; and ye shall have tribulation ten days: be thou faithful unto death, and I will give thee a crown of life.'

So I encountered 22 years and 10 months of refining and the Lord has not allowed me to suffer any loss at all. Instead I have received the greatest of blessings.[2]

Watchman Nee (1903–1972), China

In 1952 Watchman Nee was imprisoned for his faith by the Chinese government. He remained in a labour camp until his death twenty years later. In the book *The Martyrdom of Watchman Nee*, Newman Sze writes:

Many of Brother Nee's fellow prisoners wept at the mention of his name after their release. These Christians explained, 'There was never a saint like him. Bibles were unavailable, and whenever he had the chance to be alone with us, Brother Nee would hold our hands and recite a few verses and pray with us.' Prophetically, in the earlier days of freedom, Brother Nee often encouraged young people to memorize the New Testament. He said, 'The day will come when they will take away the Bible from our hands, but they cannot take away the Bible from our hearts.'[3]

Watchman Nee became a Christian at the age of 17 and began writing and speaking about his faith almost immediately. He settled in Shanghai in 1928 and established the Shanghai Gospel Bookroom, which published his own work and Chinese translations of books by English-speaking authors. As a result of his work before his arrest, approximately four hundred local churches were started in China.

On one occasion, when he was visiting Hong Kong, he was advised not to return home because of the persecution he might face. He replied: 'If a mother discovered that her house was on fire, and she herself was outside the house doing the laundry, what would she do? Although she realized the danger, would she not rush into the house? Although I know that my return is fraught with dangers, I know that many brothers and sisters are still inside. How can I not return?'

During his years in the labour camp, only his wife was allowed to visit him. She died six months before him so it was her eldest sister who was informed of his death.

His grandniece recalled:

In June 1972, we got a notice from the labor farm that my granduncle had passed away. My eldest grandaunt and I rushed to the labor farm. But when we got there, we learned that he had already been cremated. We could only see his ashes . . . Before his departure, he left a piece of paper under his pillow which had several lines of big words written in a shaking hand

. . . 'Christ is the Son of God who died for the redemption of sinners and resurrected after three days. This is the greatest truth in the universe. I die because of my belief in Christ. Watchman Nee.'

When the officer of the labor farm showed us this paper, I prayed that the Lord would let me quickly remember it by heart . . .[4]

Since his death, more than 2,300 churches have been started which trace their roots to the ministry of Watchman Nee and his co-workers.

Chapter 2

A new martyr for a new millennium

Persecution and long prison terms, such as that faced by Samuel Lamb, Allen Yuan, Wang Ming Dao and Watchman Nee, are not confined to history. In 2000, the martyrdom of 21-year-old Liu Haitao was reported by his pastor. The pastor's report was translated by the Christianity and China Research Center, Taipei for Christian Solidarity Worldwide.

Liu Haitao (1979–2000), China

Liu Haitao's pastor writes:

> As we enter a new millennium, in a period of 'reform and opening', people are seeking to pursue spiritual and material interests. In this so-called 'nation of religious freedom', thousands of Christian believers are being persecuted for their faith. They are often arrested without warrant, detained in police detention centres, beaten, and then sent to 'labour educational camps' (a form of prison where people are sent for hard labour without due process of legal trial). Christians who meet outside the official church or conduct training can be sentenced to this kind of labour camp for one to three years, especially if they do not pay heavy fines of around a year's salary. As 'prisoners' they are treated cruelly and often worse than those in the prison. Some of them are persecuted to death just for being faithful to God.
>
> Brothers and sisters in the West, believe it or not, persecution against Christians really does happen daily in the People's Republic of China. I will tell you a true story that happened very recently, which touched my heart deeply.

A new martyr for a new millennium

By the roadside of a pitched country road in Jiyang Village, stretching to Xiayi County, in Henan Province, in central China, a coffin was placed for three days prior to burial. From 16 to 19 October 2000, cars, motor vehicles, and villagers on bikes and on foot passed by and saw the coffin. They were all talking about the story. Many of them were moved to tears; some of them commented that the world is truly in darkness now. They knew that a young man was tortured to death because he believed in the Lord Jesus Christ and lived an exemplary life. Others were mocking and gossiping about it. However the family of this unburied young man was filled with deep sorrow. What happened to that young man, you may wonder?

The name of the dead young man was Liu Haitao. He was born in Liu Fang Lou Village, Ji Yang Town in Xiayi County on 24 June 1979. He was 21 years old when he became a martyr for the Lord. Liu finished school in 1996. Even during his childhood, it was his practice to kneel down and learn how to pray with his mother. He became a born again Christian in the spring of 1999. He attended a 'young believers training program' in his local House Church.

The local House Church believes in historic Christianity: it believes in the Triune God: Father, Son, and Holy Spirit, the virgin birth, the crucifixion of Christ, His resurrection, His ascension and His second coming. It also observes Christmas and Easter and practises Holy Communion and the fellowship of the believers. It follows the teachings of the Holy Bible. The believers live devout lives, love China and never interfere with the application of state laws or educational policies.

Since attending the training program, Liu Haitao grew close to the Lord. He studied the Bible very conscientiously. His spiritual life grew rapidly and his spiritual gifts abounded.

His faith was very strong and his piety moved a lot of brothers and sisters. In a devotional letter he wrote: 'By His unlimited great love, the Lord saved me. He leads me to eternal life and entitles me to become a son of God. How can I ignore His salvation and freely accept His grace without doing something for him in return? More than 90 per cent of people in China don't know God. My heart is broken. If the Lord is going to use me, I am ready to give my life to Him and start the journey of serving Him.'

Liu Haitao and 26 other believers were arrested on 4 September 2000 while they were having fellowship at a training location. They were put in a jail in Qinyang City in Henan Province, where Liu Haitao stayed until 27 September 2000.

Although life in jail was very hard for Liu Haitao, he was strengthened by the love of God and often encouraged his fellow believers in the jail. He gave his small portion of food to others, believing that to love God is to love your brother. Liu Haitao's actions deeply moved the other brothers.

On 27 September 2000, the Public Security Bureau [police] in Qinyang contacted all the county officials in the areas where the detainees lived. Officials from those counties were to take the detainees back with 'Release Cards'. After receiving the notification, the police in Xiayi county brought the detainees back, but instead of releasing them, they charged them with participating in illegal religious activities and put them in a police detention centre again.

Liu Haitao and other brothers were among those taken to Xiayi county and charged with 'practising heresies to interfere with the execution of the law of the state'. They were put on trial again in their local county. A Detention Card was issued to the family on 28 September. The Public Security Bureau asked Liu's family to pay RMB 5,000 (US$600) in exchange for his release. This is not a small amount for the peasants in this poverty stricken area in China. Liu's family could not produce such an amount, and so Liu was kept in jail. One young man's father visited his son in the jail and learned that his son had been interrogated and severely beaten and had vomited blood. The villagers were furious, but they could do nothing but surrender to the authorities.

Life in a Chinese jail is hard. The jailers torture detainees severely. Liu Haitao had a history of kidney disease. He suffered a relapse while in custody and fainted several times in the five or six days before he died. During that time he asked for medical treatment, but none of the officials in the labour camp cared. Other prisoners also begged [an] official that Liu should be treated, but the jailer said: 'There is no problem for him. He will not die. He is living a heavenly life on earth'. Not until Liu Haitao was dying did the jailer tell Liu's father to visit his son in the afternoon of 14 October 2000. Liu's father hurried to the jail. On seeing his son's grave condition, he begged prison officials for medical treatment, but the authorities said that there were rules that the prisoners were not allowed to go out for treatment during the night. If someone had money, they gave it to the jail doctor and let him treat the prisoner as needed. So Liu's father gave RMB 100 (US$12) to the jail doctor and went back home.

Early in the morning of 15 October, Liu's father went back to the jail and asked for hospital treatment for his son. The jail authorities said, 'We do not have a car for your son so you will have to rent one yourself.' Then Liu's father called a tricycle [rickshaw] to go to the hospital. At that time Liu hardly had strength to walk. In addition, he had heavy shackles of several kilos attached to his feet. Liu's father carried him to the tricycle, accompanied by the jail doctor, and they went to the hospital. On the way to hospital Liu's father asked Liu if they had given him any treatment the night before. Liu responded: 'No, no injection, they only let me take several pills.' The jail doctor knew that he had not done what should have been done and that Liu was really in danger and he returned RMB 90 to Liu's father.

After the examination in hospital, they knew that Liu Haitao was in a critical condition and needed immediate medical treatment. The police realised that Liu Haitao might be dying and began to make swift arrangements for his release in order to free themselves from responsibility. It was not until 5:00 p.m. that Liu Haitao's shackles were taken off. The PSB gave Liu Haitao a 'Release Card' without any comments.

That same night Liu Haitao died. Before he died, he told his mother with peace and joy: 'Mum, I am very happy, I am fine. Mum, just persist in our belief and follow Him to the end. I am going now, Mum. Pray for me.'

Liu Haitao leaned close to his mother's chest and when she

prayed for him, he said a very weak but clear 'Amen' and died.

The next day, the parents brought back the body of their son, who had died just a few hours after his release. In that coffin lay a young contemporary martyr for God in a country that claims to have 'religious freedom'.

On 17 January 2005 the Compass news service reported that a new law governing freedom of religion in China was to take effect on 1 March 2005. The report said:

> The New China News Agency characterized the law as 'a significant step forward in the protection of Chinese citizens' religious freedom'. New provisions may help Christian believers cut through often impenetrable bureaucracy when applying for official registration and could safeguard religious property rights. One article grants permission for churches to establish social service projects such as kindergartens, orphanages and clinics. However, improvements are more than offset by new provisions to punish members of unregistered religious groups. It also appears that religious believers outside the state-controlled church were not consulted while drawing up the law. Thus, tensions between the state and China's rapidly growing religious communities are likely to be exacerbated.

Chapter 3

Finding Christ in a human hell

The Democratic People's Republic of Korea (DPRK), known around the world as North Korea, was governed by Kim Il Sung from 1948 until his death in 1994. Since then, his son Kim Jong Il has been the head of state. Amnesty International and other human rights organizations accuse North Korea of having one of the worst human rights records of any nation. Most freedoms are severely restricted, both inside the country and abroad. According to Open Doors, Christianity is regarded as one of the greatest threats to the regime's power. The government will arrest not only the suspected dissident but also three generations of his family to root out the 'bad influence'.

According to an Open Doors report, at least twenty Christians in North Korea were arrested for their faith in 2004. It is believed that tens of thousands of Christians are suffering in North Korean prison camps, where they are faced with cruel abuses. Though no exact figures can be given, Open Doors staff discovered that more than twenty Christians were killed by open-air shootings or by beatings in the prison camps in the year 2004/05.

As Christians, we are required to:

> Speak up for those who cannot speak for themselves,
> for the rights of all who are destitute.
> Speak up and judge fairly;
> defend the rights of the poor and needy.
> (Proverbs 31:8–9, NIV)

This mandate to speak up for the poor and the vulnerable and to speak out against injustice is manifestly relevant to the dire situation in the Democratic People's Republic of Korea today.

As a parliamentarian with a deep concern for human rights, I had been outspoken in my criticisms of Kim Jong Il's brutal totalitarian regime, both in the House of Lords and the United Nations Human Rights Commission in Geneva. However, if advocacy is to be effective, it is important to try to hear all points of view, so that one cannot be accused of partiality and prejudice. My colleague Lord Alton had been equally vociferous in his condemnation of North Korea's human rights record. We agreed on the importance of a visit, if we were able to obtain visas. We were surprised when these were forthcoming.

During preliminary meetings with the North Korean ambassador in London, we emphasized that we would not tolerate any use of our visit for propaganda purposes, warning that any attempt to do so would result in our public dissociation from their representations – which would destroy any significance of the visit for us and for our North Korean hosts.

A programme was agreed in advance, which was honoured by our hosts. It included visits to churches in Pyongyang: a Protestant church for me and a Roman Catholic church for David Alton. I was surprised to find nineteen pastors from South Korea attending the service at the Protestant church; they were equally surprised to see me. One of them was preaching when he suddenly saw me in the congregation, whereupon he nearly fell out of the pulpit, exclaiming in astonishment, 'There's Baroness Cox! She has preached in my church in Seoul! What is she doing here?' Equally surprised, I asked what they were doing there and I was encouraged to learn that they were opening a Protestant seminary.

The Roman Catholic church was less well attended and the Mass could not be celebrated because there was no priest in Pyongyang. Three lay members led a service with prayer and the 'Ministry of the Word' including Bible readings and a homily, but had to omit the sacramental part of the Eucharist.

It was illegal to take Bibles into North Korea. However, we suspected that our luggage would not be searched! We therefore took a number of Bibles in Korean with us. At the end of official meetings, such as those with government ministers, we would stand to say our farewell and add a little ceremony. Holding a Bible upside-down I would say: 'Your Excellency, this is a very important book in our parliamentary tradition. We begin every day's proceedings in the House of Lords and the House of Commons with a reading from this book. We would like to offer you this as a gift – as a sign of respect as a fellow-parliamentarian.'

They took the gifts – and thus we were able to leave Bibles in many seminal places in North Korea!

Perhaps the most surprising event occurred during our final meeting. We were to be received by the President of the Presidium of the Supreme People's Assembly of the Democratic Peoples' Republic of Korea – the top political person, under the 'Great Leader'. Before this very formal meeting, our guides and interpreters were visibly terrified. If they put a foot wrong or committed a political misdemeanour, they could pay a high price. Punishment for such 'deviations' could be harsh. They were literally sweating with anxiety as they pleaded with us, 'Please, at the end of this meeting, would you mind not giving *that book*?' We did not want to compromise them, so we agreed to their request. Then to our surprise, just as were leaving, we received a message: 'It's all right to give *that book*.'

At the conclusion of a very long and formal meeting, in the presence of innumerable VIPs and officials, our host stood to shake our hands. His words were words I never thought I would hear from the President of the Supreme People's Assembly of the DPRK:

> We know you are Christians. These are very dangerous days
> for North Korea. Please would you ask Christians in the West
> to pray for us?

These are indeed still very dangerous days for North Korea. I hope that Christians in the West will not let that request for prayer from one of North Korea's most influential leaders fall on deaf ears.

Among other unexpected occurrences were our meetings with representatives of humanitarian aid organizations, including the World Food Programme, World Vision and Concern. They were cautiously optimistic that the situation was opening up and there was less manipulation of aid for political purposes. However, since then, I have tried to facilitate a much-needed health care programme under the auspices of Merlin (Medical Emergency Relief International), only to find that the situation has deteriorated and access by new aid organizations has been severely hampered.

We are also still deeply concerned over continuing reports of gross violations of human rights. While in North Korea we raised concerns over the unknown fate of two Christian pastors: Revd Ahn Seung Wun, who disappeared in 1995, and Revd Kim Dong Shik, who disappeared in January 2000. We received no reply.

On our return to Britain, we decided to establish the first-ever British–North Korean All Party Parliamentary Group to build a bridge, for two reasons: to encourage those in the DPRK who do want to try to maintain open dialogue; and to enable us to raise our continuing concerns over human rights violations. We also invited the President of the Presidium of the Supreme People's Assembly, Kim Yong Nam, to instigate a comparable visit to the UK, which took place in March 2004.

On the return visit, the delegation of four was led by Choe Thae Bok, the Chairman of the Supreme People's Assembly, the most senior North Korean official ever to have visited western Europe. As well as visiting the London Eye, the Imperial War Museum, the British Museum's Korea Gallery, and of course the Palace of Westminster, we met the Archbishop of Canterbury, Dr Rowan Williams, at Lambeth Palace, where issues of religious freedom in North Korea were raised yet again.

My deep concern over the question of religious freedom in North Korea is fuelled by the testimonies I have heard from those who have suffered for their faith in that totalitarian society. I have also entertained another Korean guest in the House of Lords.

Soon Ok Lee (b. 1947), North Korea

Former Communist Party worker Soon Ok Lee survived detention in a prison labour camp from 1987 to 1992. She endured the horror of water torture and still suffers from the physical side effects.

I had the privilege of meeting Soon Ok Lee in London soon after she had managed to escape from North Korea. After spending several hours with her, I was deeply impressed not only by her dignity, courage and graciousness, but also by her physical attractiveness: chic, slim and beautiful. When I complimented her on her beauty, she looked taken aback. 'No, I'm not beautiful,' she exclaimed; 'look at the side of my face, which has been crushed where a prison guard stamped on my head.'

I looked, and there was the evidence – one side is indeed disfigured – but I had genuinely not noticed.

'You are beautiful,' I repeated. 'Your face is so radiant with your love and serenity that your disfigurement is invisible: your spirit shines through you with a beauty which is real and compelling.'

Soon Ok Lee was not sent as a prisoner to the labour camp because she was a Christian, but for some quite different 'offence'. While she was suffering the horrors inflicted on all the prisoners, she became interested in Christianity because she could not understand how Christians could be the happiest prisoners in the labour camp. Although they were given the worst jobs and worked in the most dangerous areas, Christians would sometimes volunteer to take punishment for offences of others and would sing to God when they were being beaten. It was the consistent witness of these Christians that led Soon Ok Lee to become a Christian.

In her testimony to the US House of Representatives Committee on International Relations on 30 April 2003 she wrote:

. . . I defected from North Korea in February, 1994, with my son and I arrived in Seoul in December 1995. From 1987 through 1992 I was in the political prisoner camp of Kaechon. In addition to this statement, I would like to formally request that my additional written testimony be submitted into the record of this hearing.

Human rights are a universal criterion to measure and evaluate the political and social development of mankind. Today, human rights are most violated and least tolerated in North Korea, a blind spot of the world. Worst of all, the crimes against humanity that have been perpetuated in North Korea for decades have destroyed the humanity and personalities of all North Koreans.

The personality cult of the leaders, the father and son, was the norm that came to replace respect for humanity. To achieve this purpose, the North Korean leadership operates secret concentration camps and prisons for political prisoners in at least 12 locations. Their goal is to eliminate all forms of opposition. Over 200,000 innocent victims, including women and children, are detained there for life without a judicial process. The secret concentration camps and all forms of prisons in North Korea are the sites of the worst crimes against humanity in the 21st century.

Some 6,000 prisoners were in the Kaechon Prison when I was imprisoned there . . . All the prisoners were deprived of all forms of human dignity. From the moment of imprisonment, prisoners are treated as being lower than beasts. I experienced a living hell there during the seven years that I was there. The ordeal at that time was to such an extent that even today I am not sure whether I am alive or merely dreaming.

Kaechon Prison was one of the first prisons constructed by the North Korean regime for political offenders. As the economic situation rapidly deteriorated and food shortages became widespread in the 1980s, even petty commercial offences, such as buying or selling food in the black market, were treated as political crimes. Consequently, large numbers of innocent citizens were sent to prisons as political prisoners. Kaechon Prison was only for men until 1982. After 1982, the increase in the number of women arrested for trying to find daily provisions in the black market, or for traveling without an official 'pass' to find food, made it necessary for the prison authorities to accommodate women prisoners in Kaechon Prison.

Some 2,000 housewives were serving prison terms in Kaechon Prison when I was there. The women were typical victims of the North Korean political system. They were arrested while trying to find food when the government discontinued food rations. The women's appeals were considered an expression of political discontent and they were sentenced as political prisoners. Many of them did not have knowledge of the charges against them or what their sentences were. In prison, they found out for the first time that they had been given sentences of 10- or 15-year terms.

At Kaechon Prison, the prisoners were forced to work 16 to 18 hours daily without a moment of rest. They were only allowed to use the toilet 3 times a day at fixed times. 100 grams of poor quality corn per meal was the standard meal and often this was even further reduced to 80 or 30 grams per meal for any poor job performance or if a prisoner failed to meet the daily labor quota. As a result of these small and inadequate meals, long and hard work and lack of exposure to the sun, all the prisoners suffered from malnutrition and all kinds of diseases.

We were allowed to sleep for only 3 to 4 hours daily. Our cells were about 6 by 5 meters and contained 80 to 90 prisoners per cell. The cells were so crowded that the prisoners slept with the feet of the next prisoner right under their noses. There is only one window in each cell and it was like being in a steam bath in the summer days. In the winter, the cell was not heated so it was very cold with icy winds coming through the cracks of the floor and the window.

The prisoners are not allowed to talk to one another or to sing and were ordered by the guards to answer their questions only. The punishment is very severe for violating any prison rule. The punishment cell is most dreaded by prisoners. It is 0.6 by 0.7 meters and 1 meter high; literally a pigeon hole. Prisoners are stripped to the skin in the punishment cell. This is why the prisoners called the punishment cell 'the killing chamber'.

Pregnant women were unconditionally forced to abort because the unborn baby was also considered a criminal by law. Women in their 8th or 9th month of pregnancy had salt solutions injected into their wombs to induce abortion. In spite of these brutal efforts, some babies were born alive, in which case the prison guards mercilessly killed the infants by squeezing their necks in front of their mothers. The dead babies were taken away for biological tests. If a mother pleaded for the life of her baby, she was publicly executed under the charge of 'impure ideology'.

Human biological testing took place once or twice a year. I witnessed such tests. Some women prisoners were so hungry that they ate dirt and many died from this. In the labor factories, when there was a power outage, the women prisoners were forced to manually pull the motor belts of their sewing machines because the daily quota had to be met no matter what. Prisoners had to cleanse their crimes by working hard. The goal of the prisons is to work the prisoners slowly to their death through extremely hard work and inhumane prison conditions.

In Kaechon Prison there were many Christian prisoners. In North Korea, the North Korean leaders, Kim Il Sung and his son Kim Jong-Il, are to be worshipped as living gods. Christians had to suffer all kinds of harsh and degrading treatment in Kaechon Prison for their belief.

I am asking the international community including the United States to please intervene in this situation as a matter of international responsibility, by asking the North Korean authorities, as a first step, to respect human rights and to close down their political prisoner camps. I believe that international intervention can help this situation by demanding that the North Korean regime respect the human rights and dignity of the North Korean people.

I have submitted additional written testimony documenting the horrible treatment of innocent people in the North Korean political prisoner camps, and I am also submitting a

written memo about current information about North Korea
to this Committee. Thank you for giving me the opportunity
to testify, and I would be glad to answer any questions that
you have.[1]

Soon Ok Lee has told her story to numerous audiences including the US House of Representatives and the United Nations.
Her life is now devoted to revealing the atrocities still being
experienced by prisoners in North Korea.

Chapter 4
Known to God

Although I have not visited Vietnam or Laos, I am aware of the persecution faced by Christians in these countries. Many are known only to God. To show that they are not forgotten, we include the story of Nguyen Van Thuan of Vietnam together with details of the persecution faced by Mr Khamchan and Mr Vangthong from the Bru tribe in Laos.

Nguyen Van Thuan (1928–2002), Vietnam

Cardinal François Xavier Nguyen Van Thuan of Vietnam, who could have become the first Asian pope, was considered a man of simple faith who had suffered for his beliefs. The President of the Pontifical Council for Justice and Peace, one of the few Asians to occupy two top Vatican posts died in Rome in 2002 at the age of 74.

He spent thirteen years in prison and under house arrest in his homeland after the communists came to power in 1975 following the Vietnam War. During his years in prison, eight of which were spent in solitary confinement, Van Thuan wrote down his thoughts on spirituality, survival and hope.

In a lecture given in Los Angeles shortly before he died, he said:

> From the very first moment of my arrest, the words of Bishop John Walsh, who had been imprisoned for twelve years in Communist China, came to my mind. On the day of his liberation Bishop Walsh said, 'I have spent half my life waiting.'
>
> It is true. All prisoners, myself included, constantly wait to be let go. I decided then and there that my captivity would not

be merely a time of resignation but a turning point in my life. I decided I would not wait. I would live the present moment and fill it with love. For if I wait, the things I wait for will never happen. The only thing that I can be sure of is that I am going to die.

No, I will not spend time waiting. I will live the present moment and fill it with love.

Alone in my prison cell, I continued to be tormented by the fact that I was forty-eight years old, in the prime of my life, that I had worked for eight years as a bishop and gained so much pastoral experience and there I was isolated, inactive and far from my people.

One night, from the depths of my heart I could hear a voice advising me: 'Why torment yourself? You must discern between God and the works of God – everything you have done and desire to continue to do, pastoral visits, training seminarians, sisters and members of religious orders, building schools, evangelising non-Christians. All of that is excellent work, the work of God but it is not God! If God wants you to give it all up and put the work into His hands, do it and trust him. God will do the work infinitely better than you; He will entrust the work to others who are more able than you. You have only to choose God and not the works of God!'[1]

Reporting his death, the Catholic news service CathNews said:

In one of his books, he recalled how his jailers often asked him why he was usually so happy and he would reply: 'Because I have faith in my God.'

And his faith was infectious. He taught one of his jailers to sing the liturgical song 'Veni, Creator Spiritus' (Come, Holy Spirit). One day when Van Thuan fell into depression, the Communist guard sang it for him in perfect Latin, boosting his spirits.

Van Thuan was released in 1991 but while he was visiting Rome, the Vietnamese government declared him *persona non grata* and said he could never return home.

He became a cardinal in February 2001 and ever since was touted as a possible successor to Pope John Paul.[2]

Khamchan (b. *c.* 1946) and Vangthong (b. *c.* 1974) (sentenced to three years in prison, 2005), Lao People's Democratic Republic

Communists took over the landlocked country of Laos in 1975. After the takeover, the authorities expelled foreign missionaries, closed churches and imprisoned many Christians without trial.

In July 2002, the government issued Decree No. 92, on the Management and Protection of Religious Activities in the Lao People's Democratic Republic. The Decree was meant to assure the international community of the government's intent to improve conditions for religious minorities. However, the wording of the decree was so vague that many critics felt it would hinder, rather than improve, freedom of religion.

Compass News reported that twenty-four Christians from the Bru tribe in Laos were arrested at the end of March 2005, among them two men named Khamchan, 59, and Vangthong, 31.

'The Christians were beaten when they refused to sign an affidavit to give up their faith,' said the source, who asked to remain anonymous. 'They were also tied to a post under hot sunshine without shirt or food for one or two days, and red ants were poured on their bodies. Two of the believers – a man and a woman – were also beaten badly by the district prosecutor.'

Some of the prisoners were stripped from the waist up, bound with rope and left in a jungle area infested with red ants for several hours, according to reports from Christian Aid Mission.

Christians in Huayhoy Nua and Kaeng Aluang villages wrote a letter of appeal to the office of the Lao Evangelical Church (LEC) in Vientiane describing what had happened. An English translation of the letter states that three district officers came to their villages on 10 March in order to 'promote and propagate state and party policy'.

The officials told villagers they must 'stop and denounce their faith in Jesus religion. Every family and everyone must sign the affidavit to give up their faith and if not, we will never go back to our offices and we will base ourselves in these two villages for three to six months.' The officials also said villagers would not be permitted to leave their homes to work in their plantations and rice fields until they had signed the affidavit. Most Christians refused to sign the affidavit and more district officers, police and soldiers arrived.

On 27 March, the first two Christians were arrested at Huayhoy Nua village. Eight Christians were arrested on 28 March, seven on 30 March and another seven on 1 April, bringing the total to 24.

In their letter to the LEC, the Christians of Muangphin stated, 'We . . . therefore make an appeal to you for our right and justice, because this has not happened for any other reason than our faith.'

Christian Aid's sources reported that on 2 April, those arrested were asked to place their thumbprint on a document stating that they had renounced their faith in Jesus. Sources say officials whipped the Christians' hands, slapped their faces and pulled their hair to persuade them to sign the documents. Twenty-two of the prisoners 'signed' the documents and were set free.

One of the believers who renounced his faith later wrote a letter confessing his shame: 'I could not endure any longer while I was in the woods, so I signed the document to renounce my faith.' He then stated, 'The reason I signed the document . . . was that I was afraid . . . From now on, I declare that I believe in God.'

In July Christian Aid reported that Khamchan and Vangthong had been sentenced to three years in prison on charges of possessing illegal weapons. According to Christian Aid's contact in Laos, 'Christians commonly have been charged with social crimes, such as possession of weapons, in order to divert attention from the real issues behind arrests and imprisonment.' Such seems to be the case with Khamchan and Vangthong, the Christian Aid report stated.

The person who did possess the weapons used to accuse the two men later confessed his guilt to authorities, yet Christian Aid's contact says that 'officials refused to listen because they desire to keep Khamchan and Vangthong in prison'.

It is thought that Khamchan may have been targeted because he had been a village chief and member of the local Communist Party in Phin district before he became a Christian. When he became a Christian, he was sacked from the Communist Party leadership.

Khamchan and Vangthong are believed to have been in Muang Phin district prison since their arrests. All other Christians arrested at the same time as the two men appear to have been released.

The
Soviet Era

III

Chapter 1

The high price of revolution

Persecution of Christians was a hallmark of the Soviet era. Many were martyred, but the very fact that the era has ended gives hope to other saints living under persecution in other parts of the world today. These chapters tell the stories of some who died, and others who suffered and survived Soviet persecution. They are examples of the many whose lives have demonstrated the truth of Jesus Christ's assertion that even the powers of hell cannot overcome the Church he has established (Matthew 16:18).

I visited Russia in 1990 for the first independent Human Rights Conference to be held in the USSR. We were hosted by local people in their own homes. A colleague and I were invited to Leningrad to stay with a family in their apartment, which was already overcrowded by Western standards, with a married couple, their son and a grandparent all living in cramped conditions with two bedrooms, a living room and a tiny kitchen. They all moved into one bedroom and left the larger room for my colleague and me.

The graciousness of their hospitality humbled us. We find, again and again, that the poorest people are the most generous – and we often do not know the sacrifices they make for us. One evening our hostess, Olga, cooked chicken for dinner. It was the only time she cooked meat – and we noticed that we were the only ones around the little table to be given the meat. The next morning, trying to be helpful, as we rushed out to the conference, I asked Olga not to make any effort to cook for us – we would be very happy with 'just some bread and cheese'. Her face fell – and I realized, too late, what a mistake I had made, as she involuntarily exclaimed, 'I don't have any cheese and I have no idea where I can get any.' I tried to undo the damage – in vain. That night, there was bread and cheese for us and I do not like to think how long it took her to find that cheese in those empty shops and how much it cost her in those days of shortages unimaginable to those of us coming from the affluent West with our well-stocked supermarkets.

On the last evening in Olga's home, she and her husband Victor played us records of their sacred music – the beautiful liturgy of the Russian Orthodox Church. They also showed us maps of Leningrad marked with blue and red crosses, with the red crosses far outnumbering the blue. The red represented all the churches destroyed by Stalin; the few blue crosses were the only ones which remained. The next morning, as we sat round her little breakfast table, Olga stood and proposed a toast.

'Thank you for coming here,' she said. 'You have brought us hope. You have shown us it is possible to live in a land where people still smile. Here in the USSR, we cannot smile. When I or my husband go to work, or Sergei goes to school, we cannot smile, because we don't know whom we can trust. But you have given us a vision of a world where people do smile and I pray we may find that vision comes true for us one day.'

I had to reply with another toast. Feeling deeply humbled, I responded: 'You have given us a much greater gift and a much greater vision. I think when God looks down from heaven, you make him much happier than we do. We in the West ought to smile: we have so much. We have our freedom and we have food in our shops. But you have shown us how you have kept a flame of light burning even in the darkest days and kept the faith in spite of persecution and suffering. Thank you for giving us that vision to take back to the West. It is far greater than anything we have been able to give you.'

That day I learned an important lesson. Never to fail to appreciate those precious gifts we in the West tend to take for granted: freedom to worship; to meet and talk with friends without the fear of the watching eyes or listening ears of secret police, incurring reprisals for us – or, even worse, for others; and the freedom to go shopping in stores where there is the additional freedom of choice between an array of goods on well-stocked shelves.

To put the stories of Soviet saints and martyrs into their

historical context, here is a potted history (with apologies to historians for such a simple summary of this significant era). Briefly, the Soviet Union was formed after two landmark events: the Russian Revolution of 1917, which overthrew the provisional government, and the Bolshevik victory in the Russian Civil War of 1918–20, which ushered Lenin into power. Joseph Stalin took over from Lenin in 1924 and consolidated his authority with widespread arrests and executions.

More than 95 per cent of all churches were closed under Stalin and his aggressively anti-religious campaign. Some 20,000 churches were reopened in the 1940s, but most of them were closed again under Khrushchev's leadership (1953–64). Stalin's cruel policies also led to the enforced dislocation of the Armenian people, when he cut off part of historic Armenia and relocated it as an isolated enclave in Azerbaijan. In a later chapter, we will return to stories of people caught up in the brutal, bitter war which has raged in and around Nagorno Karabakh as a result of Stalin's ruthlessness.

Ann Shukman of the Keston Institute writes:

> The Brezhnev years (1964–82) saw little let-up in the oppressive nature of the regime. Andropov became head of the KGB: there were a series of political trials; for the first time psychiatric hospitals were used as places of detention. Prague was invaded in 1968, Afghanistan in 1979, Solzhenitsyn was hounded and eventually expelled in 1974, and Andrei Sakharov, the outspoken defender of human rights, was exiled to Gorky in 1980 . . .
>
> The death of Brezhnev in 1982 and the accession of Andropov brought a new clampdown, more arrests, directives against contacts with foreigners, harsher conditions in the camps . . . But darkness comes before the dawn . . .[1]

After the brief rule of Chernenko, Mikhail Gorbachev became leader of the Soviet Union in 1985 and, Shukman writes, 'at the end of 1986 came a sudden change . . . Sakharov was summoned back from exile, and a year later preparations were in full swing for the public national celebration of the millennium of the baptism of ancient Russia in June 1988. Christianity became officially acknowledged as a valued part of Russian heritage.'

Gorbachev's introduction of *glasnost* (openness) gave the people new freedom, such as freedom of speech. Reporting restrictions were removed and public debate on every issue became possible.

Writing an open letter to Mikhail Gorbachev in 1987, Michael Bourdeaux, founder of the Keston Institute, urged the Soviet leader: 'Build a new creative relationship with religious believers. After seventy years of state atheism, constant pressure and even persecution, they are nevertheless both a dynamic and a growing force in Soviet society. They are a major sector of the workforce. They do not want to overthrow: they want to construct something better from within. They have immense potential, given encouragement, to transform the social face of the land. They care. They care intensely for their fellow human beings: they care for the values of society.'

In 1989 the first open elections since 1917 were held and the following year the Soviet Union began to disintegrate as its constituent republics declared their independence.

On 25 December 1991 the red flag was lowered from the Kremlin. By the end of the month the Soviet era was history. But what a price had been paid! The countless numbers of people who had suffered persecution will be known only to God. But some who were well known became emblematic of the high cost of freedom. I will never forget the awe which overwhelmed me when I first visited the home of the famous Soviet academician Andrei Sakharov, the youngest man ever to be elected a full member of the Soviet Academy of Sciences, in 1953, at the age of 32 for his work in nuclear physics. His deep commitment to freedom of scholarship and freedom of speech led him to campaign publicly for such freedoms. Incurring the wrath of the Soviet authorities, he was exiled to the provincial town of Gorky, where he was kept under house arrest for several years.

He died in 1989, just before I met his widow, Elena Bonner, early in 1990. She invited me to stay in her apartment, and to sleep on a sofa in the room which had been Andrei Sakharov's study. She had kept it as he had left it – with his watch still ticking on his desk, surrounded by his papers and many of his most famous books.

I could not sleep, thinking of the privilege of finding myself in a room which had been the place where one of the most famous fighters for freedom in the Soviet Union had written his classic works. I always associate the memory of the privilege of that time in his home with his beloved Elena Bonner, who shared the deprivations of his exile and who still maintains a passionate commitment to freedom, with the words spoken by Thucydides at Pericles' funeral oration in 431 BC: 'The secret of happiness is freedom, and the secret of freedom is courage.'

Although he was not a Christian, Andrei Sakharov was a passionate defender of human rights. He knew that truth sets people free. When Georgi Vins, a Baptist leader, was re-arrested in 1974 after serving a prison sentence, Sakharov wrote the following appeal to the World Council of Churches.

I ask you to intercede for Georgi Petrovich Vins, the well-known religious figure, the Baptist, who was elected by his fellow-believers as Secretary of the Council of Evangelical Christian-Baptist Churches.

Vins, like other members of his family, has several times been arrested and subjected to other illegal persecutions. Recently he has been compelled to hide from the threat of another arrest. In March 1974 Vins was arrested in Kiev and charged with vagrancy. Protesting against this arbitrariness, he has already for more than four months been on a hunger strike which is threatening his life. The trial is expected in the coming weeks, and he is once again threatened with a prison sentence. Vins enjoys enormous authority and love among his fellow-believers. By interceding in his defence you will be helping all the Evangelical Christians-Baptists who have now been persecuted for many years by the authorities in the worst traditions of religious intolerance of the Middle Ages and of the Tsarist authorities in the time of Pobedonostsev, in the 1890s.

The arrests, breakings-up of prayer meetings, fines, discrimination in schools and at work, and, as the height of inhumanity, the taking away of children from their parents – all this is the lot of the Baptists and to one degree or another of many other religious groups who are inconvenient to the authorities (Uniates, Pentecostals, members of the 'True Orthodox Church' and several other groups).

These illegalities demand the intervention of the world-wide public. Freedom of conscience is an individual part of freedom as a whole. Honest people throughout the world should defend the victims of religious persecutions wherever these take place – in tiny Albania or in the vast Soviet Union.[2]

Many Russians have demonstrated the same commitment to freedom as Sakharov. Among them were countless men and women who suffered and died in prisons and the Soviet Gulag for the freedom to believe and to practise their faith.

The following two stories, contributed by Ann Shukman of the Keston Institute, outline how the Soviet era began by making martyrs.

Grand Duchess Elizabeth Fedorovna, née Elizabeth of Hesse (1864–1918), Russia

In the summer of 1918, with the outbreak of civil war, the Bolsheviks sent members of the Russian royal family eastwards deep into the heart of Russia. But in July an unexpected threat came from the anti-Bolshevik Czech Legion in the east and the prisoners were hastily executed: on 17 July the former Tsar Nicholas with his wife Alexandra and their five children were killed in Ekaterinburg, and on 18 July at Alapaevsk, a hundred miles away, the Grand Duchess Elizabeth with her companions met a particularly horrific lingering death.

Elizabeth ('Ella') was the daughter of Ludwig IV of Hesse and his wife Alice, daughter of Queen Victoria. At the age of twenty she married Grand Duke Sergei Aleksandrovich, the brother of Tsar Alexander III. Ten years later her younger sister

Alix became the wife of Tsar Nicholas II. Elegant, beautiful, intelligent and socially at ease, Elizabeth shone in Russian society and her adopted country warmed to her. After six years of childless marriage, she converted to Orthodoxy, finding there a faith that was to sustain her through an unhappy marriage and the tragedies to come. In February 1905 her husband, then Governor of Moscow, was blown up by an assassin. His wife knelt in the snow to gather the fragments of his body on the street.

The shock of the assassination had a profound effect on Elizabeth. She changed from being a woman of the world to one whose whole life was dedicated to Christian service. Having visited her husband's assassin in prison and forgiven him, she sold all her jewels and her fine collection of furniture and paintings and with the proceeds established in Moscow a pioneering community of religious women dedicated to serving the poor. The Martha–Maria community, of which she was the inspirational mother superior, became the focus of the rest of her life. Because women in religious orders in Russia were traditionally not active in charitable work outside their convents, the novelty of Elizabeth's foundation was that all its sisters, who became known as the Sisters of the Cross of Love and Mercy, went out to work with the poor, the sick and the needy and were medically trained to do so. With their distinctive pale grey habits they became familiar figures in the roughest districts of the city. In all but name the sisters were deaconesses, but in the conservative climate of the Russian Orthodox Church at that time any suggestion of reviving the ancient order of deaconesses, which Elizabeth certainly considered, was out of the question.

The hospital in the community grounds became famous for its standards of care and the best specialists came to work there. It had an out-patient clinic, a pharmacy and a dental surgery. In addition Elizabeth organized a feeding centre for the poor, flats for young female factory workers, a clinic for women with tuberculosis, and a free library. In 1913 she provided clothes for 1,800 children. She established a boys' hostel at the Khitrovka market, and in order to give them employment she set up a boys' messenger service which gained an excellent reputation. After Vespers on Sunday open discussions about the faith were held in the community church, and these attracted many people who found no other outlet for their questionings.

At the opening of the community she addressed the women who were joining her: 'I am leaving a glittering world where I had a glittering position, but with all of you I am descending into a greater world – the world of the poor and the suffering.' She herself led the life of an ascetic, sleeping on a wooden bed without a mattress. She often slept for no more than three hours, spending the night-hours at prayer or visiting the sick. She qualified as a theatre nurse and assisted at operations. During the day she would go to the worst areas of the city, visiting basement slums and the local markets, gathering up orphans to bring to her refuge. She went without protection to areas where even the police did not dare go, believing that 'The image of God can sometimes be obscured by darkness, but it can never be destroyed.'

She hoped that branches of her community could be set up outside Moscow, but this was not to be. With the outbreak of war in 1914 and the rise of anti-German sentiment, Elizabeth and her community became the object of attacks and abuse, and with the coming of the Soviet regime it came to an end. Many people – relatives, friends, the Patriarch, the German ambassador – tried to persuade her to escape, but she refused to leave Russia.

On 7 May 1918 she was arrested with two of the sisters and sent first to Perm and then to Alapaevsk. Here she and five other members of the Romanov family were imprisoned in a school. These five included the elderly Grand Duke Sergei Mikhailovich, the three young sons of Elizabeth's favourite cousin, Grand Duke Konstantin Konstantinovich – Konstantin, Igor and Ioann – together with young Prince Vladimir Pavlovich Paley. Elizabeth organized a kitchen garden and the group read the Bible and prayed together in the evenings. During the night of 18 July the prisoners were woken up, bound and blindfolded and taken by cart to a mineshaft twelve kilometres away. First Elizabeth and then Sister Varvara

Yakovleva were thrown down the shaft, their executioners expecting them to drown in the water at the bottom, but the water was not deep and their voices could be heard. Then the men were thrown in. The assassins tossed in a grenade, followed by another. Silence, but then voices could be heard singing 'Lord, save thy people'. Having no more explosives left, the assassins stuffed the mineshaft with dry brushwood and set it alight. Still the sound of hymns rose up through the black smoke until on the following day nothing more was heard.

When the bodies were discovered three months later by the White Army they found that Elizabeth had been tending and bandaging the young Grand Duke Ioann. The bodies were exhumed and those of Elizabeth and Sister Varvara Yakovleva were eventually interred in the crypt below the Russian church of St Mary Magdalen in Jerusalem.

Elizabeth was canonized by the Russian Orthodox Church in April 1992. Her statue stands with those of the other twentieth-century martyrs on the west front of Westminster Abbey. The Martha–Maria community has been revived in Moscow and continues to operate in the traditions of its foundress.

Metropolitan Veniamin of Petrograd (1874–1922), Petrograd, Russia

On the night of 12/13 August 1922, at an obscure wayside station outside St Petersburg, four men faced a firing squad. Before the execution they had been shaved and dressed in rags so that the soldiers would not recognize them for who they were. The bodies were hastily buried in a nearby grave which has still not been identified. So ended the life of the 49-year-old Metropolitan of Petrograd, Veniamin Kazansky, and his associates: Archpriest Sergei Shein, who was aged 56, the layman Yury Petrovich Novitsky, professor of canon law at Petrograd University, aged 39, and the layman Ivan Mikhailovich Kovsharov, an ecclesiastical lawyer, aged 44.

Fearing popular demonstrations after the Revolutionary Tribunal had passed the death sentence on these men on 5 July, the authorities had let it be known that the prisoners had been transported to Moscow, for Metropolitan Veniamin enjoyed widespread popularity among the people of the city, and especially among the workers. During the days of the trial large crowds had stood outside the Philharmonia Hall where the Revolutionary Tribunal was sitting.

Veniamin – Vasily Petrovich Kazansky as he was in civil life – was born in 1874 into a priest's family in the remote north of Russia in Olonetsk province. As a bright child destined for the Church he quickly moved from the provinces to the St Petersburg Theological Academy and took the path of the 'black clergy' – those who vowed themselves to celibacy and who could rise to be bishops, rather than that of the 'white clergy', who married and were destined to be parish priests. Under the Tsarist regime he rose to be bishop of Gdov in 1910 (suffragan of St Petersburg) and unlike many of his colleagues devoted himself especially to the poor and the destitute of the city. It was from this time that he became known to the workers in the great factories on the outskirts of Petrograd, and to the slum-dwellers of the most wretched parts of town. He regularly visited the outlying and neglected parishes of the city. No one who sought an audience with him was turned away, and to all he offered comfort and encouragement. Veniamin was not known as a great orator or a great theologian and he did not interest himself in Church politics, but when he spoke or preached it was with words of gospel simplicity which all could understand. He won wide respect and affection as a pastoral bishop.

When in February 1917 Nicholas II abdicated and the Provisional Government took command one of its first measures was to introduce elections into the structures of the Church. Veniamin, who was by far the best known of the candidates, won by an easy majority, and thus he became the first bishop ever in the Russian Orthodox Church to have been elected by the people.

But this glimmer of democracy was not to last long. With the October Revolution and the coming to power of the Bolshevik Party with a declared atheist ideology, attacks, at first sporadic and then systematic, began on the Church, which was faced with the unprecedented problem of how to continue its existence under a regime intent on destroying it. Unlike some of his colleagues who emigrated, Veniamin remained with his people, declaring his impartiality in politics, while calling for an end to all fratricidal bloodshed, and for a return to Christian principles of compassion and love for one's neighbour. The first test came in January 1918 when Commissar Ilovaisky, with armed sailors and workers, attempted to take over the Alexander Nevsky monastery, site of his apartments, his offices and of some of the city's holiest shrines. In the scuffles Archpriest Petr Skipetrov fell to a Red sailor's bullet, but the attackers withdrew in the face of the crowds who came to the defence of their sanctuary. The next day a huge religious procession from all the churches of the city demonstrated the strength of popular feeling. It converged on the monastery and Metropolitan Veniamin addressed the crowds:

> In these recent days our motherland that once was Holy Russia has become a catacomb for the dead. This catacomb is full of the bodies of people who move, act, and speak, but who are dead to faith, dead to patriotism, dead to love and compassion for one's neighbour, to the voice of conscience . . . They thought that by granting freedom to licence and to human passions, by promising all earthly goods, by showering money, that they would force people to forget heaven, forget God, forget conscience. But these means can never achieve such ends. Dearly beloved, you who once were our brothers, children of one family, remember that you cannot fight with God, you cannot uproot faith. Persecution of the faith only strengthens it. So it was, so it will be and so it is now.

The mass demonstration in Petrograd passed off peacefully, which was not the case elsewhere. But the Soviets realized that brute force alone would not destroy the churches and in the next few years they turned to other methods.

The Soviet government's new law of January 1918 on the separation of Church and state took away from the Church the right to own property and opened the way for the confiscation of Church premises, and the takeover of schools, charitable institutions, and other Church premises. In Petrograd, however, thanks to the initiatives of Veniamin, the faithful organized themselves into parish soviets and brotherhoods under a single Petrograd Brotherhood of Parish Councils. These organizations cared for the poor and needy in their areas, and formed pressure groups to withstand the demands of the government. Veniamin, aware that he still had widespread popular support, but sensing the hardships to come, did all he could at this time to encourage the next generation in the faith. It was a period of numerous conversions, especially from among the intelligentsia. Veniamin encouraged youth work and children's associations. The diocese organized mission work in the rural areas around the city, and for a time, the Brotherhood of Parish Councils even took back from the Soviets the theological institutions which had been confiscated.

Ahead of his time, Veniamin sought to engage other Christian denominations in the defence of religious rights, but the window of opportunity for Church activities was closed by the late summer of 1918. In the months to come, the authorities launched a new and more brutal onslaught on religious life. Then in the autumn of 1919 the threat of the White Army, which was approaching Petrograd, intensified attacks on the clergy in that city. The clergy were thought to support the White Army, though most, under Veniamin's lead, remained in Petrograd and stayed politically neutral.

Through these policies and his consistently apolitical stance Veniamin was able to maintain some vestiges of Church life in his diocese through these first years of the Soviet regime. But the Soviet government changed tactics in its aim to eradicate every trace of religion and seized on the opportunity of the terrible famine in the Volga regions in 1921–22 to blackmail the Church and so to weaken it. While the general popular climate naturally favoured giving all possible help to the starving, the authorities could seize Church valuables on the grounds that if the Church is so full of Christian compassion, then it could willingly yield its valuables to help the starving. Probably unaware at first of the hidden agenda, Veniamin responded immediately: 'The Orthodox Church obeys the teaching of Christ the Saviour and always serves as an example of selfless love at a time of calamity.' At a meeting with the city Party authorities on 5 March 1922 he came to an agreement to give all that the Church possessed, and won permission for two Church representatives to oversee the melting down of the valuables and the purchase of grain for the starving.

This was not, however, what the central Party authorities wanted: they were seeking pretexts for violence. Soon new instructions came from Moscow that the Church valuables were to be immediately taken by force. Veniamin responded at once: on 12 March he declared that forced confiscation would be blasphemous and all who assisted in such acts would be excommunicated. A few days later news came through of bloodshed at Shuy during Church confiscation, and the Petrograd public prepared to resist the armed officials when they approached the city churches. Outside some of them skirmishes broke out. This was enough for Veniamin and his clergy to be accused in the press of counter-revolution and anti-Soviet actions. Once again Veniamin called on his faithful not to have recourse to violence and reminded them of Christ's words that 'my kingdom is not of this world'. In other cities where the clergy led the resistance to the confiscations this was used by the authorities as a pretext to arrest them and close down the churches.

While Veniamin was prepared to be conciliatory towards the Soviet authorities over a question of material possessions, when it came to the question of the structure of the Church and his loyalty to Patriarch Tikhon, now under house arrest in Moscow, he was resolute. In the early months of 1922, a group of Petrograd clergy, at the direct instigation of the GPU (the security services), formed a splinter group known as the 'Renovationists' or 'Living Church' with the aim of working closer with the Soviet authorities. In May 1922 they established a Higher Church Administration which was to bypass the Patriarchate and take over its functions. This was the first example of what was to become standard Soviet policy, namely to split religious groups from within.

For Veniamin this disloyalty was a step too far. On the day of Pentecost, 28 May 1922, in spite of threats to his safety, he publicly denounced these Renovationist schismatics. Soon afterwards, the leader of the Renovationists, Fr Alexander Vvedensky, a one-time protégé of Veniamin's, came with the security services to search Veniamin's apartment and to arrest him. He approached Veniamin to ask for his blessing, but Veniamin refused, saying, 'Father Alexander, we are not in the garden of Gethsemane.'

Metropolitan Veniamin, along with 85 others, clergy and laity, were accused of long-standing counter-revolutionary activity. The show-trial, the first of many which the Soviets set up, began on 10 June in the Philharmonia Hall. If the aim of the Revolutionary Tribunal was to break Veniamin, they did not succeed. He stood by his own innocence and that of his fellow-accused. On 4 July, reminding his accusers that he had been elected by the working people of the city, he spoke his final words:

> Now for the second time I am being judged by the people's representatives. I am not guilty before those workers who have sent you here to try me. I am apolitical, I live only for the interests of the Church and the people, and in all things I obey the Lord's will. Neither are the other accused guilty . . . Whatever sentence you pronounce, I shall know that it is pronounced not by you but that it comes from the Lord God, and whatever befalls me I shall say: Glory be to God.

Fear of popular demonstrations prompted the Revolutionary Tribunal to execute Veniamin in secret, dressed in rags with his beard shaved, so the firing squad would not know the identity of the man they were executing.

On 31 October 1990 the Presidium of the Supreme Court of the Russian Federation annulled the sentence passed by the Petrograd Revolutionary Tribunal in 1922 on the grounds of insufficient evidence. In April 1992 Veniamin and his three companions were canonized by the Russian Orthodox Church and a memorial to them has now been erected in the cemetery at the Alexander Nevsky monastery in St Petersburg.

Chapter 2
Suffering – a Soviet family's inheritance

> The Spirit himself testifies with our spirit that we are God's children. Now if we are children, then we are heirs – heirs of God and co-heirs with Christ, if indeed we share in his sufferings in order that we may also share in his glory.
>
> (Romans 8:16–17, NIV)

None of us want to see our children suffer, yet for Soviet Christian families who have refused to deny their faith, suffering has been the inheritance handed down from generation to generation.

Peter Vins (1898–1943), Russia

In 1932, while in prison for his faith, Peter Vins wrote this poem to his four-year-old son Georgi:

> Now you are forced involuntarily
> To suffer for the name of the Lord,
> But I pray that you may willingly
> Choose the thorny path of Christ.
>
> When the golden days of childhood
> Have passed by, and as a young man,
> You turn your clear eyes
> Into the lands of your dreams,
>
> Then give up all your strength of will,
> All the dreams of your heart,
> Your unpolluted life and destiny –
> Everything to His service![1]

Born in Samara – called Kuibyshev during the Soviet era – Peter Vins went to the US for theological training then returned to work as a missionary in Siberia. From 1926 to 1930 he served as a pastor in Blagoveshchensk-on-Amur in the Far East.

His first arrest in 1930 led to a labour camp sentence. At the time, Vins was representing the Brotherhood of Evangelical Christians-Baptists of the Far East at an assembly in Moscow. On his arrival in the city he was summoned to the NKVD – the People's Commissariat for Internal Affairs, as the Soviet secret police was called. They advised him to support the government's candidates for membership of the Baptist Union board. He refused to accept government interference in Church affairs and within a few days, he was arrested. Peter then spent the next three months under investigation in prison before being sentenced to three years in a labour camp. On his release Peter did find work, but it was not easy for an ex-convict; evenings were devoted to encouraging and comforting other Christians in Omsk, where the family settled.

After his second arrest in 1936, the investigation into his alleged 'crimes against the State' took nine months. However, Peter and his eleven co-defendants were finally acquitted when the witnesses retracted their evidence and told the court how they had been threatened and intimidated during the investigation. At the end of the trial the judge said to Peter: 'You are a man with education, but you concern yourself with faith – dope!' Peter replied: 'I beg you not to insult our faith! Faith in God is the purpose of life!'

Peter Vins was arrested for the last time in 1937, convicted in a closed court and sentenced to ten years in a labour camp without the right of correspondence. Ten years passed and he did not return home. His family later discovered he had died on 27 December 1943 at the age of 45 in one of the Soviet labour camps. He was posthumously rehabilitated twenty years later as a result of his wife's petitions.

In a letter which did reach home, Peter wrote: 'Tell our dear ones to pray that the Lord will strengthen the brethren and myself to be His faithful witnesses. It is doubtful that I will be released, although our only crime is faithfulness to the Lord. It is better to be with Him in prison than at liberty without Him.'

Georgi Vins (1928–1998), Russia

As a child in the winter of 1937 Georgi Vins watched convoys of prisoners as they passed his house. Years later he wrote: 'Unshaven faces, lean faces . . . I went out into the street and searchingly scrutinized the prisoners' faces; it seemed to me that I was just on the point of seeing my father's face among them. But he was not among the convoy passing by.'

Like his father, Georgi also emerged as one of the leaders of the Reform Baptists. He too was arrested and held in solitary confinement in a KGB investigation cell in Lefortovo prison – one of about thirty Christians in the prison in 1966. Recording events of 1966 in *Faith on Trial in Russia*, Michael Bourdeaux wrote:

> June, July, August, September . . . All these months Georgi Vins, Gennadi Kryuchkov and almost all their closest associates, who had been arrested together . . . underwent the peculiar rigours and mental torture of a Soviet pre-trial investigation . . . Their grandfathers had sown the seeds of the faith and been persecuted under the Tsars; their fathers had been persecuted under Stalin; now it was their turn under Khrushchev and his successors. Already the laurel wreath of martyrdom was being prepared to hand on to their children in their turn. Throughout all this, however, God had given them strength and not failed them.[2]

When Georgi Vins and Gennadi Kryuchkov, came before the court in November 1966 very few other Christians were admitted to the court; instead the duo faced a hostile audience. The trial lasted from 10 a.m. to 9 p.m. on the first day and 10 a.m. to 1 a.m. the following day and night. Vins and Kryuchkov were exhausted when they came to make their final speeches. We begin with a transcript of Georgi Vins' address to the court.

Suffering – a Soviet family's inheritance

Vins: I want to say that I consider myself fortunate to be able to stand here and testify that I'm in the dock as a believer. I'm happy that for my faith in God I could come to know imprisonment, that I've been able to prove and strengthen myself. I do not stand here as a thief, a brigand or as someone who has infringed the rights of another person. I stand before you with a calm and clear conscience; I have honourably obeyed all the civil laws and faithfully respected the laws of God.

I thank God that I've been able to experience the great joy of hearing a witness from Siberia say that he considered me his brother in the blood of Jesus Christ. After this recognition I'm prepared to accept any sentence passed by the court.

In the presence of my wife, I want to offer thanks to God that He has revealed to me the truth of the teaching of Jesus Christ and that I am a Christian. I am glad that for two days I've been able to speak before all these people. Some of you hadn't the patience to hear us out – there were grins, laughter and noise.

I do not see you, Comrade Judge, Comrade Prosecutor and all here present, as my enemies; you're my brothers and sisters in the human race. When I leave the courtroom, I shall pray to God for you there in my cell, asking that He should reveal His divine truth to you and the great meaning of life. [*Shouting and laughter in court*]

But here, too, there are my brothers and sisters in the blood of Jesus Christ. You are dear to me. The Bible alone has been my preceptor; it has taught me to be upright. For us Christians no prisons are needed.

Judge [*interrupting*]: By law one should not interrupt a defendant when he's delivering his final address, but you're delivering a sermon, you know. Don't forget what audience you're addressing.

Vins: I consider that in my final speech I must be given the opportunity of expressing all that's in my heart. In conclusion, I want to say:

The Soviet era

Not for robbery, nor for gold
Do we stand before you.
Today here, as in Pilate's day,
Christ our Saviour is being judged . . .

Once again abuse resounds,
Again slander and falsehood prevail;
Yet He stands silent, sorrowfully
Looking down on us poor sinners.

He hears the sorry threats,
He sees the trepidation of those people,
Whose hands have gathered tears
Of children, wives and mothers.

Forgetful of history's lessons,
They burn with desire to punish
Freedom of conscience and of faith
And the right to serve the Lord.

No! you cannot kill the freedom of belief,
Or imprison Christ in jail!
The examples of His triumphs
Will live in hearts He's saved.

A silent guard binds round
The friends of Christ with steel ring,
But Christ Himself inspires us
To stand serene before this court.

No rebel call has passed our lips,
No children offered as a sacrifice;
We preached salvation constantly,
Our message one of holy thoughts.

We call upon the Church of Christ
To tread the path of thorns,
We summon to a heavenly goal.
We challenge perfidy and lies.

And so we stand before you,
Or rather, have been forced to come,
So you can learn the ways of God,
That sons of His stay true to Him.

Fresh trials now and persecution
Will serve alone to strengthen faith
And witness God's eternal truth
Before the generations still to come.

At this point, uproar broke out in court once again, but this time the judge took it upon himself to quell it. He gave Vins no chance to continue.

Gennadi Kryuchkov was then instructed to make his final address to the court, in which he said:

Those brethren who are at this moment in prisons and camps are suffering, not for having broken Soviet law, but for having been faithful to God and his Church. They're suffering for Christ, who called them to a new life. Some of them are reformed criminals. Thanks be to God that this was when they were of the world, but when God touched their hearts they selflessly followed after him. Now they are ready to give up what is their own, but not to appropriate what belongs to others . . .

. . . I'm happy to stand before you as a Christian. I'm glad that the court has not proved we've committed any offences, so if you observe the law we shall be liberated from imprisonment at once. But if you act in accordance with the prophecy of Jesus Christ about his followers, 'They will also persecute you' then we shall be sentenced . . .

This court hearing has astonished me, but I'm glad to be associated with the company of those who've gone to prison.[3]

The transcript of the trial concludes with these words: 'The court proceedings ended at 1 a.m.'

'The court sentenced Brother G. K. Kryuchkov and Brother G. P. Vins to three years' imprisonment to be served in "special regime" camps.'

In 1971 Michael Bourdeaux wrote this verdict on the court proceedings:

> 'Soviet justice' had done its worst. Georgi Vins and Gennadi Kryuchkov had received the maximum sentence under the relevant article of the Penal Code. But that was just about the only legally normal aspect of the trial. It was conducted before a public gallery baying for the blood of the defendants, and set out to do little less than render the accused physically incapable of defending themselves. The verdict was brought in at one o'clock in the morning. Such is the lot of the Christian in the Soviet Union today who will in no way compromise his faith.
>
> All the other leaders of the Reform Movement and very many of their most prominent sympathizers were sentenced at about the same time. We have the trial transcripts of a few others, and from these we can see that the treatment meted out to Vins and Kryuchkov was no better and no worse than the others received, except that not everyone was given the maximum sentence. Hundreds of these people are no more to us than names on a list, but they were not forgotten by their friends, relatives and sympathizers left behind.
>
> Nadezhda Vins watched her husband being led away from the dock. He disappeared from sight, but he and Kryuchkov did not disappear from the minds of those who continued to pray for them during the long imprisonment ahead. Indeed, those sentenced provided a source of inspiration for the future activities of those still free.
>
> Nadezhda Vins was left to cope with four children of school age. This would have been a difficult enough task, even if she had continued to earn her former good salary as a highly qualified translator of foreign languages. But, according to the usual Soviet practice, punishment was extended to the relatives of the convicted man. She lost her job and had to take up a menial task – employment as an ice-cream seller.[4]

Vins' health deteriorated in prison, but he refused the offer of early release by the KGB in return for cooperation with them against the Church. By the end of 1969 Vins was taking an active part in the Council of Churches once again. Restrictions and state interference continued, forcing Vins into hiding for three years, working clandestinely as a pastor. His mother was arrested in 1970 and sentenced to three years in prison and Vins was re-arrested in March 1974, then held incommunicado for the next six months. His eldest daughter was dismissed from work as a doctor in a Kiev hospital: religion and medicine were incompatible, she was told.

Vins was sentenced to five years in a labour camp, followed by five years of internal exile. But the appeals from around the world on his behalf had an impact, leading to his dramatic expulsion from Russia after he had completed the first five years of his sentence. He died in exile in the United States on 11 January 1998 at the age of 69; he had been suffering from a brain tumour. His funeral was held in his adopted home of Elkhart, Indiana, where his Russian Gospel Ministries was based.

Chapter 3
Holding fast to faith

In 1973 Aleksandr Solzhenitsyn's book *The Gulag Archipelago* alerted the world to the conditions faced by prisoners in these 'corrective labour camps' or 'special-regime camps' as they were called. Soviet labour camp life was unbelievably hard. Food rations were never adequate. Severe weather, long working hours and, often, physical abuse by camp guards meant many inmates died from exhaustion, brutality and disease.

I had a tiny insight into Siberian life when I was invited to receive an honorary doctorate from the Siberian State Medical University in the once-closed city of Tomsk. Tomsk was at the centre of a TB epidemic in Russia when Medical Emergency Relief International (Merlin) first sent a three-man evaluation team in 1994. Tuberculosis was increasing in the former Soviet Union at a rate of 10 per cent a year and a quarter of those infected were expected to die. There were 75,000 new cases in Russia that year alone. I went to Tomsk with the Merlin team, who went on to develop a TB control programme in Siberian prisons. When we visited one prison, we greeted some of the prisoners, who stared out at us from tiny barred cell windows. The guards were surprised. No one ever speaks to them, we were told. As well as seeing first hand the dehumanizing experience of prison life, we were bitten alive – the summer air is full of mosquitoes. With Siberian winter temperatures of –40 and mosquito-infested summers, everyday living conditions can be incredibly harsh. Labour camp conditions endured by these Soviet saints and martyrs are unimaginable.

The outspoken Russian Orthodox priest Fr Gleb Yakunin – elected in 1990 to the Russian Congress of People's Deputies – was among the many who endured the brutal conditions of Soviet labour camp life.

Gleb Yakunin (b. 1934), Moscow, USSR

Father Gleb Yakunin was one of the leading figures in the religious renaissance in Russia. I had the privilege of meeting him in Moscow in the early 1990s. I immediately felt I was in the presence of a spiritual giant. His rugged face reflected the strength and integrity which had underpinned his resistance during the long years of Soviet communism. But there was also a compassionate tenderness and the occasional twinkle in his eyes, which indicated that this was no fanatic zealot, but a man whose deep faith, love and passion for truth had taken him down the road of resistance and sustained him throughout the ordeals of persecution. It is these characteristics which motivate his continuing refusal to countenance any kind of compromise – even in the relative freedom of the post-Soviet era.

Fr Gleb came to international attention in 1965 when he and another young Orthodox priest appealed to the Patriarch Alexi of Moscow – the leader of the Russian Church – to take a more resolute stand against state interference in Church affairs. Perhaps his best-known appeal is the one he co-authored and sent to the Fifth General Assembly of the World Council of Churches in Nairobi in 1975. This document provoked the first serious examination by the West of religious persecution in the USSR, according to the Keston News Service.

Fr Gleb, born in 1934, was ordained a priest at the height of the Khrushchev anti-religious campaign in August 1962. In 1976 he and two other Orthodox believers founded an unofficial group, the Christian Committee for the Defence of Believers' Rights in the USSR, which set itself the task of advising and assisting believers of all denominations and documenting violation of these rights and Soviet legislation on religion.

During a new wave of repressions against believers, Fr Gleb was arrested on 1 November 1979 and held incommunicado until his trial at the end of August 1980. He was tried for alleged anti-Soviet agitation and propaganda though all his activities had been within the framework of Soviet law and the rights enshrined in the Soviet Constitution.

The outcome of the trial was patently predetermined. Witnesses were called selectively, as several who had been summoned to appear and had intended to express support for Fr Gleb were not admitted into the court. The judge refused to allow Fr Gleb to explain the activities of the Christian Committee, even though the documentation issued by the Committee formed the basis of the charges. Fr Gleb refused to plead guilty. Yet the trial was not without its surprises. For example, one witness, a churchwarden whose dubious activities had been exposed by Fr Gleb, had been confidently expected to vilify him in her testimony. To everyone's amazement she stated, when called to the stand, that although she had had differences with Fr Gleb, she considered him to be a true Christian, a man of impeccable integrity, an example to all and someone she was proud to know. No amount of favourable testimony, however, could change the outcome of the trial. Fr Gleb was sentenced to five years' strict regime camps with five years' subsequent internal exile. In his final word to the court, Fr Gleb stated simply: 'I rejoice that the Lord has sent me this test. As a Christian I accept it gladly.'

Fr Gleb's appeal against the sentence was rejected in March 1981 and he was sent to a labour camp. In a letter smuggled out of the camp Fr Gleb said that his Bible had been confiscated by camp authorities. His wife had ensured that the Bible he took with him to camp was one printed in the Soviet Union under the auspices of the Moscow Patriarchate. Fr Gleb wrote in a letter dated 21 June 1981 (from camp) that he intended to commence a protest fast on 16 September in order to get his religious literature back. It was learned in November that he had been moved to the camp hospital and had been fed intravenously since 26 September. He was sent back to labour camp and ended the hunger strike.

It was not the end, of harassment, however. Family visits were cancelled, although he was entitled to three visits a year. He was deprived of the right of correspondence but was able to let his family know that he was in good spirits and glad to suffer for the sake of Christ. During the second half of 1982 he spent four months in solitary confinement in the internal prison of the labour camp, with very low food rations, no correspondence and a 'bed' on the floor of the cell. The official reason given for this harsh treatment was that he had engaged in 'religious agitation' or among the young inmates. At other times he was placed in a punishment cell for trying to come to the aid of fellow prisoners who were being beaten up. On occasion such beatings were carried out as provocations to force Fr Gleb to come between the guards and a victim, in order to place him in detention for interfering with the guards.

Then suddenly in July 1983 the Moscow Patriarchate arranged for him to have a pastoral visit, to receive communion and a Bible. This, according to his friend and co-member of the Christian Committee Vadim Shcheglov, was a piece of window-dressing to divert any possible protest on Fr Gleb's behalf at the World Council of Churches General Assembly in Vancouver beginning on 24 July. During the Assembly, the Archbishop of Canterbury, Dr Robert Runcie, sent a message to the Soviet leader, Yuri Andropov, requesting that steps be taken to allow Fr Gleb's family to visit him. Numerous appeals on his behalf were made by religious and human rights groups around the world.

On 14 March 1987, the *New York Times* printed a short notice that Fr Gleb had been released from Siberia by the Supreme Soviet (on 13 March) and that he was returning to Moscow after ten years of exile for being a founding member of the Christian Committee for the Defence of Believers' Rights in the USSR. However, he did not abandon his efforts to speak up for the rights of Christian believers.

Writing in *Rebels and Reformers*, Trevor Beeson reported:

In 1990, however, he was elected to the Russian Congress of People's Deputies and with two other priests founded the Russian Christian Democratic Movement, becoming joint chairman of its Parliamentary group. At the end of 1994 the Bishops' Council decreed that his political activities were contrary to canon law and when he refused to give up his seat in Parliament he was unfrocked, though he continued to wear his clerical robe and pectoral cross.[1]

As this book was being compiled Fr Gleb was still active in Russian politics as a member of the Public Committee in Defence of Freedom of Conscience.

Fr Gleb Yakunin was one of the survivors among many saints who were sentenced to years in prisons and labour camps. Some were martyred in detention; others died after their release. From 1973 to 1983 the Keston Institute journal *Religion in Communist Lands* reported on the situation of believers in the Soviet Union and Eastern Europe and in 1983 Carolyn Burch compiled a list of those known to Keston College who had died in that period under the Soviet regime. Their brief biographies are stark, a simple memorial to the many who died. Not all of the stories end on a note of triumph, but they all highlight the high price these saints have paid for an unswerving commitment to their Christian faith.[2]

Ivan Moisevevich Ostapenko (? –1974), Baptist, USSR

The presbyter of Shevchenko Evangelical-Christian Baptist congregation, Ostapenko was serving a three-year term of exile, following a four-year prison sentence under Articles 209 and 138 of the Ukrainian Code. He had been given the opportunity to serve his exile nearer his home on condition that he renounce his beliefs, which he refused to do. On 26 January 1974 he was found hanged in the basement of a house; his family, refusing to believe the official verdict of suicide, wrote a letter of protest to Brezhnev.

Ivan Vasilievich Biblenko (1928–1975), Baptist, USSR

Biblenko was a leader and preacher from Krivoi Rog who had served a three-year term in a strict regime camp under a sentence imposed in 1972. On 13 September 1975 he set off to a church meeting in Dnepropetrovsk, and failed to return. His family, after extensive and fruitless enquiries, were finally informed of his death in hospital on 24 September, allegedly due to injuries sustained in a road accident. Accounts given of the 'accident' were not satisfactory, and after examining his body his relatives were convinced that 'he died as a result of torture'.

Raisa Ivanova (1929–1977), True Orthodox, USSR

Sentenced for belonging to the True Orthodox 'sect', Ivanova refused to work in the Mordovian camp in which she was interned. In October 1974 she was declared mentally ill and transferred to Kazan Special Psychiatric Hospital, where she suffered severely from the intensive treatment she received. At the end of 1977 she hanged herself.

Starets Tavrion (1898–1978), Russian Orthodox, USSR

Born Tikhon Danilovich Batozsky, Starets (spiritual counsellor) Tavrion spent 28 years (1928–56) in camps and exile. In 1957 he was made abbot of the Glinsk Hermitage, but this was closed a year later and he spent the next eight years serving in various dioceses. In 1968 he replaced Starets Kosma as spiritual father of the Hermitage of the Transfiguration near Riga. Thousands of pilgrims came there from all parts of Russia to hear his spiritual teachings. Tavrion died, after many months of suffering from cancer, at the age of 80.

Zenon Adamovich Kalienuk (1887–1979), Uniate, USSR

Kalienuk, Dean of the Ukrainian Catholic (Uniate) Church, was arrested in 1946 and sentenced to long-term imprisonment for refusing to change his faith to that of the (officially sanctioned) Russian Orthodox Church. He was arrested again in 1974 for demanding the re-establishment of the Ukrainian Catholic Church, and suffered continual persecution until his death in the spring of 1979.

Tatyana Karpovna Krasnova (1903–1979), True Orthodox, USSR

Tatyana Krasnova died at the age of 76 while serving the sixth year of a sentence, under Article 70, of nine years' imprisonment and three years' exile. This was her second prison term: she had already served one in Kengir from which she was released in 1955.

Vladimir Andreyevich Shelkov (1896–1980), Seventh-Day Adventist, USSR

Shelkov, who became the leader of the True and Free Seventh-Day Adventists in 1954, embodied the courageously uncompromising conviction of this group that it is contrary to Christian conscience to profess loyalty to the atheist state or to submit to state registration. He spent twenty years of his life in prisons and camps. In 1969 he founded the unofficial Adventist publishing house True Witness, through which he produced many works on the question of the state and religion, including an eight-book series under the title 'The Just War for Freedom of Conscience against the Dictatorship of State Atheism'. Shelkov was last arrested on 14 March 1979, and sentenced to five years' strict regime labour camp – the sentence produced a wave of protests both in the USSR and in the West, but Shelkov died in the camp, aged 84.

Semyon Bakholdin (1929–1980), Seventh-Day Adventist, USSR

A member of the True and Free Seventh-Day Adventist Group led by Shelkov (see above), and also involved, with Shelkov, in the Adventist Group for Legal Struggle, Bakholdin was arrested in 1978 and sentenced to seven years' special regime camp to be followed by three years' exile. (He was accused of trying to avoid military service by means of bribery.) He lost the use of his legs due to being confined in damp prison cells, and died during the second year of his imprisonment, aged 51. Since relatives were unable, despite repeated attempts, to have access to his body, it was suspected that his death was not entirely from natural causes.

Nikolai Petrovich Khrapov (1914–1982), Reform Baptist, USSR

Khrapov died at the age of 68 following a heart attack in a labour camp near Shevchenko in the Mangyshlak region of Kazakhstan. He had been an outspoken evangelist in the unregistered Evangelical Christian and Baptist churches since 1971, and spent a total of 28 years in prison camp and exile. In the camps he brought many fellow-prisoners to faith, the best known of whom was the former criminal Vasili Kozlov.

Chapter 4

Karabakh – keeping the faith in a struggle for survival

The collapse of the Soviet Union took everyone by surprise. In its aftermath, there was chaos in many of the countries which emerged into independence, particularly the south Caucasus region, which includes three disputed areas: Abkhazia and South Ossetia in Georgia and Nagorno Karabakh in Azerbaijan.

My attention has been focused on Armenia, which lies not only on a geological fault-line, prone to earthquakes, but also on a geopolitical fault-line, where West meets East and where oil interests run deep. It is also one of the places where Christianity meets Islam, although it must be emphasized that the war which erupted in the early 1990s in the tiny, predominantly Armenian enclave of Nagorno Karabakh was not a religious conflict. As Andrei Sakharov put it in 1989: 'For Azerbaijan the issue of Karabakh is a matter of ambition; for the Armenians of Karabakh, it is a matter of life or death.'

To understand the significance of the present, it is essential to know a little of the past. As the history of the region is permeated with conflict, any account will inevitably be partial and I must therefore put my own credentials in context.

I first heard of Karabakh during the Andrei Sakharov Memorial Congress in Moscow in May 1991. Chairing a group of experts on human rights, I met, as another member of this group, one of Karabakh's elected deputies to the Supreme Soviet of the Soviet Union. He spoke in great detail of major violations of human rights being inflicted on the Armenians living in and around Karabakh, including systematic deportations of villagers, in which entire communities were driven off their land, in brutal operations accompanied by murder, torture and pillage. These operations were part of a policy designated Operation Ring, comprising the proposed ethnic cleansing (a term used in relation to Azerbaijan's policy before it became familiar to the world in the context of the former Yugoslavia) of all Armenians from their ancient homeland of Karabakh.

As chairman of this group, I was asked by the Congress to lead an independent, international delegation to the region to ascertain the facts. We were truly independent, with no preconceptions or prejudices. We met many of those who had suffered deportation. We also walked across the border into Azerbaijan to meet Azeris in one of the areas where fighting had already begun, to hear the Azeri viewpoint. We were deeply concerned by our findings and decided to return as soon as possible, via Azerbaijan, to obtain more evidence of Azeri policies being pursued in Karabakh and to obtain a more systematic representation of Azerbaijan's position.

We wrote reports detailing all our findings. These, together with a fuller analysis of the history of the conflict and details of evidence obtained during many subsequent visits, are available in the publication *Ethnic Cleansing in Progress: War in Nagorno Karabakh.*[1]

After those two initial visits, the members of the international independent delegation came to the conclusion that Azerbaijan was the primary aggressor and that its policy of attempted ethnic cleansing of the Armenians was a gross violation of human rights. Subsequently, in the autumn of 1991, Azerbaijan announced its intention to annul Karabakh's autonomous status and to rename its capital city with a Turkish name. The Armenians saw this as the beginning of the end for their survival in this little land, which has been historically Christian since Armenia became the first nation to embrace Christianity, in AD 301. Some of the oldest churches in the world are found in Karabakh – such as the fourth-century church and monastery in Amaras, where the visitor can still see a tombstone dated AD 430. The small Armenian population resorted to the only constitutional right they could exercise in the rapidly disintegrating Soviet Union: they held a referendum and obtained an overwhelming mandate for self-determination.

Azerbaijan responded with a full-scale 'military solution' to the 'problem' of Karabakh. As 1991 drew to an end, the 150,000 Armenians in Karabakh became the victims of ferocious military offensives by seven-million-strong Azerbaijan. It was a war of

David against Goliath. When I returned in January 1992, I flew into one of the most intense conflicts of the 1990s. The Armenians of Karabakh were surrounded, blockaded, bombarded. Azerbaijan had cut off their electricity, and was pounding the capital city, Stepanakert, with a blizkrieg by day and night. Women and children were immured in basements and cellars; with no electricity, they had no light, heat, running water or sanitation. The doctors had no medicines, so there were no anaesthetics or pain-killers for the casualties of war. When I visited the basement hospital, I met a lady who had suffered amputation of both legs – with no pain relief – but she never complained. All she kept saying was 'Thank you for coming. Thank you for caring enough to be here.' I could not sleep at night thinking of so many men, women and children enduring such unrelieved pain. So began our regular missions to Armenia and Karabakh during the dark days of that terrible war.

Later that month, when I returned with a consignment of medicines, the bombardment had intensified. The Azeris were now using Grad multiple-missile rocket launchers against the civilians in Stepanakert and surrounding villages. I used to count 400 Grad missiles every day pounding in on Stepanakert (forty missiles in each volley and ten rounds a day, beginning at 7 a.m.).

I discovered in those dreadful days that Christianity runs deep, not only in the soil but also in the souls of the Armenian people. As part of Stalin's Soviet Union, they had suffered ruthless persecution, with the execution or deportation to the death camps of the Gulag of all their priests and the destruction or closure of all their churches. However, as the Soviet Union disintegrated and the Armenians of Karabakh began fighting for survival, the first bishop to return came back into that hellhole to be with his people.

Bishop Pargev Martirosyan (b. 1954), Nagorno Karabakh

During my second visit in January 1992, I was in Stepanakert when Bishop Martirosyan's house received a direct hit from a large bomb. He had been in bed (the only place, in those bitter days, where anyone could be warm, with temperatures at minus 20, and no electricity to give any heat or light.) But as soon as the shelling began, he immediately got up to pray. Within one minute, the bomb hit his house – and a large concrete slab fell directly onto the bed where he had been sleeping. There was a case of a man whose life was literally saved by prayer!

Bishop Pargev Martirosyan, Primate of the Artsakh diocese of the Armenian Apostolica Church, is a man of considerable intellect, substance and humanity, as well as a man of faith.

Before ordination he studied electrical engineering, then language and literature. He then worked as a teacher of Russian language and literature, and as an army conscript in the advertising department of Armenia's Ministry of Industry. He was ordained in 1985 as a celibate priest and continued his theological studies, receiving a doctorate in 1987. While serving as vice-chairman and lecturer at the Seminary of Holy Etchmiadzin, he was appointed abbot of St Hripsime Monastery, Armenia. In 1989 he was appointed Primate of the Artsakh diocese of the Armenian Apostolic Church and became Archbishop in May of that year.

When I visited the bishop in the ruins of his home, I asked if he would like to give a message to the rest of the world or to fellow Christians. He replied:

Our nation has again begun to find its faith [after seventy years of Soviet communism] and is praying in churches, in cellars and on the field of battle, defending its life and the lives of those who are near and dear. It is not only the perpetrators of crime and evil who commit sin, but also those who stand by – seeing and knowing – but who do not condemn it or try to avert it. Blessed are peacemakers for they will be called sons of God. We do not hate – we believe in God. If we want God's victory, we must love. Even if there are demonic forces at work, not only in this conflict, but in other parts of the world, we must still love – we must always love.

Chapter 5

Murdered or martyred?

Alexander Men (1935–1990), Russia

I am not the only one to have seen the significance of Nagorno Karabakh. Fr Alexander Men, another modern martyr, described Karabakh in his Christmas meditation in 1989 as 'a collective symbol for the innumerable tragedies which seem to be erupting one after another in so many parts of the world'.[1]

Alexander Vladimirovich Men was an immensely influential Russian Orthodox priest who was murdered on 9 September 1990. He was struck on the back of his head with an axe as he was walking to the train station on his way to his parish church in a village near Moscow. His murderers have never been identified and many see Fr Alexander as a modern martyr.

Alexander's parents were Jewish, but his mother had felt drawn to Christianity. She and her eight-month-old son Alexander were secretly baptized in September 1935 and made occasional clandestine visits to a 'catacomb priest' for confession, communion and counsel. At the time, the Russian Orthodox Church existed almost exclusively in secret, sustained by a few clergy or 'catacomb priests' as they were known.

Alexander was intellectually gifted and an avid reader. From the age of twelve he was aware of his vocation to the priesthood and, under normal circumstances, he might have taken a science degree, worked in a specialist field for a few years, then trained as a priest. But his Jewish heritage and contact with the Church meant he was denied a place at university. Instead, he studied biology at the Institute of Fur in Moscow and continued to study theology on his own under the guidance of Fr Nikolai Golubtsov, a priest at a church in Moscow.

When the Fur Institute was transferred to Siberia, Alexander moved with it and shared a room with Gleb Yakunin, who also became a priest and critic of the Church establishment. Alexander's contact with the bishop at the cathedral opposite the institute came to the attention of the authorities and, when Khrushchev launched another violent anti-religious campaign in 1958, Alexander was refused permission to sit his final exams and was abruptly returned to Moscow.

Fr Golubtsov arranged for him to be ordained a deacon and in 1960, he was ordained priest and posted in Alabino, near Moscow.

In a biographical note on Alexander Men, Ann Shukman writes:

> Alexander was now twenty-five years old, mature beyond his years, with quite extraordinary intellectual and spiritual training behind him. He was already writing his books. To his intellectual and spiritual gifts was added another, particularly important one for the life of a parish priest in times of persecution, a gift of getting on with all kinds of people. During the Khrushchev anti-religious campaign priests were forbidden to officiate anywhere outside their church buildings without official permission from the local authorities: any infringement, whether baptizing at home, conducting funerals, or giving the last rites, could be used as a means of inculpating and arresting them. Fr Alexander, however, knew how to talk to the local officials and continued to carry out all these normal functions of a priest.
>
> The Alabino period was marked by another development. At Fr Alexander's initiative, a group of a dozen young clergy of the Moscow region, including Fr Gleb Yakunin, Fr Dmitri Dudko and Fr Nikolai Eshliman, used to meet for discussion and to share experiences . . .[2]

House searches and interrogations became a feature of Alexander's life and, when he was denounced by a superior, he had to move. His pastoral and literary activity made him a target for the KGB and, for a time in the 1980s, he was called in for daily interrogations.

When, in the late eighties, Mikhail Gorbachev instituted the policies of *perestroika* and *glasnost*, there was an explosion of religious life in Russia and Fr Alexander Men was suddenly in demand as a public speaker on the subject of Christianity, making TV appearances and starting his own television series on religion. Ann Shukman writes:

> Always there was about him a sense of urgency, a sense that time was short. In spite of all the talk about spirituality nowadays, he would say, much of what passed for religion was sentimental and *ersatz*. 'Notice', said Fr Alexander, 'that no one, not even the bishops whom they produce on television, is preaching Jesus Christ, or God; they don't speak of the essentials of what we believe.' We must 'hurry to give people the authentic message of Christ', because this liberty could come to an end at any time.
>
> . . . At Easter 1990 Fr Alexander baptized 60 adults. He took part in the opening of the Bible Society in Russia, he was involved in starting a new university . . . and a cultural association . . . Many have spoken of his prayer life, the sense he had of the nearness of God and the presence of Christ . . . He had the gift of living completely in the present: everyone who spoke to him felt that he was concerned only with them in the whole world. And he had a deep sense of humour and a gaiety that sprang from his faith.[3]

The night before he was murdered he gave the final lecture in a series on world religions. He was full of optimism: the victory has already been won; new life has come and Christianity is only in its infancy, he said. Those who heard him said they had the impression that he knew his life was approaching its end: they noticed that his voice was different and that he seemed to speak straight from the heart.

Some have noted that the axe used to kill him may be of special significance. In Russian history, the axe was the weapon used to chase out foreign invaders and became the traditional symbol of popular justice, of the punishment of traitors. For many, the murder of Fr Alexander Men was no ordinary crime, though it is unlikely that his murderers will ever be known.

Africa IV

Chapter 1

Nigeria – a front line of faith and freedom

> Crucify us, torture us, condemn us, destroy us. Your wicked-
> ness is the proof of our innocence . . . The more we are hewn
> down by you, the more numerous do we become. The blood
> of martyrs is the seed of the Church.
>
> Tertullian (*c.* 160–225), *Apology*

Bishop Benjamin Kwashi (b. 1955), Nigeria

I first met Bishop Benjamin Kwashi on my first visit to Nigeria.
He welcomed me with a characteristic Nigerian smile and
warm hospitality. My visit took place soon after the Lambeth
Conference in 1998, when bishops and archbishops from the
worldwide Anglican Communion had met in Canterbury for a
very tense and troubled gathering. As our conversation ranged
over the problems being experienced in Nigeria, especially in
the states where sharia was being imposed, my mind went back
to that Lambeth Conference. I asked him whether he had felt
that the majority of bishops and archbishops there had felt any
deep concern for the church suffering persecution.

For a moment, his face lost its radiant African smile and he
looked infinitely wistful as he replied: 'No. In fact I and my
brother bishops returned to Nigeria feeling very alone.'

Then his warm, humorous African smile quickly returned, as
he said with a twinkle in his eyes: 'In fact, we felt so alone, we
turned to God to say our prayers – which, perhaps as bishops,
we should have done before. And now you have come. You
are an answer to our prayers. Will you tell the world what is
happening here in Nigeria?'

Thus began my mission and my mandate – to tell the world

what is happening in Nigeria, as well as so many other parts of the world, where men, women and children are holding a front line of faith and freedom – and often paying a high price, including the ultimate price – for so doing.

Bishop Benjamin is no stranger to persecution. His church and home have been burned by Muslim fanatics. His life has been threatened; his friends and colleagues martyred. 'If we are taken by death through persecution we would have fulfilled our mission on earth,' he says, but he is not morbid. Joy as well as sorrow shapes his life. Many people have come to know Christ through his ministry. He has worked in rural and urban churches, as a polytechnic chaplain and as rector of a theological college, becoming well known in Nigeria and beyond as an evangelist and preacher. His commitment to the gospel and to the work of mission governs all he does.

He became Bishop of Jos in 1992, having been ordained in 1982. The diocese was small in terms of numbers, finance and vision, he says. In the years since then, the geographical size of his diocese has diminished, but the number of priests has more than quadrupled – still not enough to meet the needs of the ever-growing number of churches, he adds.

Bishop Benjamin believes that sound Christian education is a vital key to the future growth and development of the Church. He has established an ever-growing number of Anglican secondary schools as well as developing training opportunities for clergy, health workers and musicians. Health care, HIV/AIDS prevention and care, plus concern for a cleaner, safer environment have also been high on the Bishop's agenda.

His wife Gloria is also a graduate in divinity, an evangelist and a community worker. Their home and family are the anchor for the bishop's life and the backbone of his ministry.

I visited Nigeria most recently in June 2005 and I can testify that the situation continues to pose challenges to the Christian communities, especially those living in the northern states where sharia has been imposed.

In addition to visiting Plateau State, where we saw at first hand the evidence of recent conflicts, we also travelled to

Bauchi State, where we met the Anglican Bishop of Bauchi, the Rt Revd Laudamus Ereaku, at St Paul's Cathedral. He described the current situation:

> In this part of Nigeria, the atmosphere has changed, as it has become more Islamic. Previously, there was peaceful co-existence in each state under the governors and emirs. Now, the Muslim fundamentalists do not want peace . . . Many of the Christians who are not indigenous have left the city, such as businessmen.
>
> In this sharia state, Christians tend to be the scapegoats. If there is a disagreement between Muslims, they tend to turn their anger on the Church.
>
> Current concerns relate to the defilement and removal of five churches; an Islamic school has been built in their place. The authorities have also built public toilets adjacent to a church; in another instance, a church is used as a cattle market – despite a Certificate of Occupancy held since 1983. When the bishop raises these matters with the authorities, they repeatedly respond with sustained procrastination.
>
> The government has set up an interfaith Religious Council, but its membership consists of twenty-four Muslims and only twelve Christians. There is discrimination in many areas, such as the university, with fewer places given to Christian applicants than to Muslims (except in subjects where it appears that Muslims do not do so well, such as sciences); there have been no new appointments of Christian staff; there is marked discrimination in the civil service, where well-qualified Christians are kept in junior positions, under less-qualified Muslims.

The bishop did however express appreciation of the governor, whom he described as fair and honourable.

On wider issues, the bishop was adamant about the need for more support for the Christians. The Muslims are receiving massive support from Saudi Arabia. For example, in Zamfara State, the first to adopt sharia, funds came from Saudi Arabia and it was recognized that this was a political as well as a religious initiative. But the Christians are not receiving any help from the government (or anyone else) because others do not consider the issue of sharia as serious.

Claiming that Islam had long ago planned a long-term strategy, the bishop said it could be seen to be developing with the destruction and/or closure of Christian schools and hospitals in the 1970s. The cathedral school land was taken away and a stadium has been built on it. The authorities took over many other Christian institutions, and renamed them – as well as renaming roads. There have been two attempts to force a change of Christian school uniforms, but these have so far been resisted.

The bishop said that his diocese has received no support from the international Christian community – from no-one, including the Anglican church. If a church is burnt, they receive no help. They have themselves tried to help those in Jos Diocese who have been afflicted, but they have to rely on self-help: 'We have not received any visit from any representatives of the Anglican church. Our only hope is in our God.' The only people who have helped the Anglican diocese in Bauchi are from one of the Dioceses in the south (in the Niger Delta); they have sent some funds for clergy.

Many problems persist. For example, during attacks on the Christian communities, the local people only had primitive weapons to protect themselves against well-armed troops – so many were killed. There are now a large number of widows and the church has established a Widows' Fund to provide small amounts of capital for them to try to establish businesses. But they suffer great problems trying to maintain their families, pay school fees, etc.

While I was in Bauchi State, we visited three churches and one pastor's house in Ganjuwa Local Government Area, which had been attacked a few months before. Local Muslims had burnt a nearby house and the police arrived in time to stop further assault, I was told.

Then, at a market nearby, people saw smoke rising; youths started rioting and shouting 'Let's go and destroy the infidels'. Although police tried to intervene, they could not prevent them from burning the COCIN (Church of Christ in Nigeria) and Roman Catholic churches and the pastor's house.

The bishop's final message is this:

> Seeing is believing. If you don't move out and come to see us, you will never be able to feel the impact of our experiences. If you just read about us, you cannot feel. If you come, you can feel and understand. If you care enough to come, you can experience our appreciation of your care for us. We ourselves need to reach out to support our people and churches scattered around the city. So if you can speak out and give us any help, we can help them. But, above all, please pray for us. We cannot run away from where we are. We thank God for the challenges we are facing. Please pray for us that God will sustain us and keep us faithful to the end.

Bishop Benjamin Kwashi told Obed Minchakpu, based in Jos for Compass News, that he believes the rise in attacks on the church in Plateau State, as well as in northern Nigeria, is based on the desire to oppress Christians politically.

'We are trying to understand why the Muslims are bent on hitting the church hard on the Plateau, because if you talk with some of them honestly, you find the reasons for the crisis have nothing to do with the church,' he says. 'They will tell you the problems are equality in political sharing of offices.'

That is, Muslims who feel their tribal or religio-cultural interests are not recognized have misdirected their frustration at the Church. 'When they want to fight for political recognition, they attack the Church, so the Church has become a scapegoat,' he adds. 'You can go through all the reasons they give, and not one is a concrete reason that the Church has offended the mosque. Not one!'

Plateau State has a population of more than 2.1 million, of whom Christians constitute well over 90 per cent. It is the only state close to northern Nigeria that has a high concentration of Christians. Mission agencies and churches in northern Nigeria have their headquarters in Jos, the state capital. Pastor Dan Manjang, director of church relations at the Nigerian Bible Translation Trust (NBTT) in Jos, is one of many Christians who believe Muslims have targeted Plateau State because it is the only state near northern Nigeria that serves as a hub for Christian missions to the Islamic north.

Pastor Manjang says Muslims in Plateau State enjoy equal rights with Christians and face no opposition to practising their faith. 'Muslims here are appointed to political positions of power. They have commissioners in the government cabinet; they have permanent secretaries in the government, their children get scholarship grants like Christian children, Muslim schools are grant-aided by the Plateau State government, and they have contested elections and won. So what are they complaining about?'

In other Islamic states in northern Nigeria, Christians are denied these privileges, Pastor Manjang points out: 'While Muslims in Plateau State get land to build mosques, build houses, etc., Christians in Islamic states like Zamfara, Borno, Bauchi, Kano, and the rest are denied land to build churches.'

Pastor Manjang, who served on the board of Plateau State Radio and Television Corporation, says Christian and Islamic programmes have equal access to airtime on radio and television in Plateau State. But in Islamic states, Christians are denied broadcast of even paid-for programmes. 'On radio and television stations in the Islamic states of Bauchi, Sokoto and Kano, you can never find a single Christian programme, yet in Plateau State, Muslims have enjoyed all these privileges.'

Manjang concludes: 'The claim of Muslims in Plateau State that they are being discriminated against is a farce.'

Christians have felt deeply worried about their response to violence perpetrated against them. On my first visit to Jos, I met the head of ECWA (the Evangelical Church of West Africa), Victor Musa. I will never forget his anguish as he agonized: 'What are we to do? We have turned one cheek; we have turned the other cheek – and we have no cheeks left to turn.'

However, reprisals by Christians may help fuel Muslim claims that they are religiously, economically, or politically obstructed. Certainly Christians have mounted counter-attacks on Muslims in Nigeria. Revd Alexander Lar of COCIN, based in Jos, says that within his denomination, 'There has never been on our side a clear attack or an open attack on anybody, except a reprisal on our attackers, because not all of us are people who will run away. There are people who want to defend themselves, and they embark on reprisal.'

Revd Lar says violence in Plateau State from 2001 to 2004 led to 173 churches being burned down. 'Eight pastors were killed. One of them had his whole family killed.'

The Plateau State chapter of the Christian Association of Nigeria (CAN) released the names of seven of the martyred pastors to Compass Direct in Jos. They are Pius Kurnap, Simon Nimbon, Aminu Lachak, Musa Fannap, Salbol Dashe, Musa Vongkur and Emmanuel Nimmak. An eighth victim, a pastor of the Deeper Life Church whose name was unavailable, was killed with his wife and four children. The ministers served Baptist, Anglican, Roman Catholic, Assemblies of God and Evangelical Reformed congregations, as well as COCIN and the Evangelical Church of West Africa.

Bishop Benjamin says Muslim attacks have brought the Church to her knees. The Anglican church alone lost sixty congregations in 2001: 'Churches were burned, destroyed, wiped out.'

Chapter 2
Martyred friends

Bitrus Adoro Manjang (1933–2002), Nigeria

Pastor Dan Manjang, director of church relations at the Nigerian Bible Translation Trust (NBTT) in Jos, lost his father, Bitrus Manjang, and members of his family to violence. A thanksgiving service planned to honour Pastor Dan's father became a family funeral when Bitrus, his daughter-in-law, who was pregnant, and his grandson were killed three days before the celebration was due to take place.

In a letter to Bishop Benjamin Kwashi, Pastor Dan gave his account of events:

> On Thursday 12 December, 2002, there was an onslaught on Rim village of Riyom Local Government Area of Plateau State in Nigeria, by Fulani militia and Muslim fundamentalists numbering well over 500! The result of this onslaught is the heinous killing of Reverend Bitrus Adoro Manjang, one-time Vice President of the Church of Christ in Nigeria (COCIN), and two members of his family – Victoria, his daughter-in-law and her son Jessy. As a matter of fact, Victoria was pregnant. The fourth member of the family, named Gyem, escaped with bullet wounds.
>
> A total of 14 persons were killed on that fateful day leaving 20 others wounded. No less than 70 houses were torched with many others pulled down . . . also grain and livestock were lost.

All those who died were buried on 21 December 2002.

In his letter to the bishop, Pastor Dan says: 'The sad thing to note is that the late Revd Bitrus Manjang was a man of peace who was loved by all. He was hacked down by the Fulani, a people whom he had shielded and protected from being killed by the youth in the village. He was totally against shedding of blood.'

Bitrus Manjang had spent five years in their home village of Rim since he retired in 1997 working for peace by housing displaced Muslims and stressing forgiveness toward violent extremists.

'There are many instances of him taking the initiative to house Muslims displaced by the religious conflict in our family house in Rim village,' Pastor Dan continues. 'This was before the village was attacked by the Muslim fundamentalists. Our house became a house of refuge for displaced Muslims.'

Pastor Manjang's father was also instrumental in the Rim church's initiative to accommodate displaced Muslims in its building. 'These Muslims were cared for by the church for over two weeks,' he says. 'Ironically, my father and the very Christian community of Rim that assisted displaced Muslims became the target of the mayhem and violent orgy of the Muslims.'

The younger Manjang says that because his father was a peacemaker, even fellow pastors hated him as they believed he was protecting Muslims who were attacking Christians. They sought counter-attacks, but he would not consent.

'He rejected the idea of revenge because he believed forgiveness is the central theme of the Christian message and wondered how this can be reconciled with the desire by some Christians for revenge.' Pastor Dan adds: 'My dad had always said his refusal to allow Christians to carry out reprisal attacks on the Muslims was because Christ talked about His followers being peacemakers.'

Revd Bitrus Adoro Manjang was born in the village of Rim and studied at Gindiri Bible School, and the Gindiri College of Theology. After his ordination in 1969 he taught in the COCIN Bible School in Foron, and went on to hold a variety of posts as part of COCIN, becoming Vice-President in 1992.

He was one of the translators of the Old Testament into Berom and had authored three books. His fourth book, to his Berom kinsmen, entitled: *Gasi ha ga ye gbei* (It is Dawn) was awaiting publication when he was killed. As well as translation work, he contributed regularly to the Hausa devotional book *Abincin Ruhaniya* (Food of the Spirit).

He leaves a widow, Garos, nine children, two stepchildren, two sisters and sixteen grandchildren.

Iyasco Taru (1953–2000), Nigeria

In February 2000, more than 2,000 people were killed in religious unrest in Kaduna, Nigeria, according to a BBC News report. One of those killed was Revd Iyasco Taru, whose martyrdom is highlighted by Bishop Benjamin Kwashi in the Foreword to this book.

Revd Iyasco Taru stands out among the many victims of violence as one who witnessed to the power of God's love and grace – even as his attackers were leading him away to be slaughtered.

He was born in 1953 into the family of Baba Taru and Mama Kwarba Kwaghe at Tudun Wada Bazza, Adamawa State, Nigeria. He became a Christian in Waka, where he attended the CBM Teachers' College, graduating in 1974. He then went to Jos for further training at the Theological College of Northern Nigeria, graduating in 1982.

Ordained in 1994 as a minister of Ekklesiyar Yan'uwa a Nigeria (EYN), the Church of the Brethren in Nigeria, his first posting was in Abuja, the fast-growing capital of Nigeria, where he and his family stayed until 2000.

Mrs Rebecca Paul Gadazama, who has compiled a record of Revd Taru's life, explains that he was transferred to pastor the EYN church in Badarawa Kaduna on 1 January 2000, moving his wife and five children to Kaduna on 9 February. Two days later he convened a district conference, during which he said many strange things implying that he had finished his race. He said similar things to his wife.

Mrs Gadazama writes:

On 20 February there was a crisis all over Kaduna. The next day some Moslem militants marched to Rev Iyasco Taru's church. They killed all his chickens and turkeys. The militants kept coming and going, considering what to do with Iyasco, his family and church properties. A Moslem neighbour did all he could to stop them from harming the church.

The next day the church was set ablaze . . . Iyasco did not leave 'the House of God on fire' as he put it. He kept encouraging his family and those around the burning church with the Word of God, referring to what was happening as the fulfilment of the Scriptures.

Early the next day, 22 February 2000, his wife insisted that they leave, since the church and their home had been destroyed. By that time the militants were going after him and his family, so Iyasco took them to shelter in a church member's house. But the militants came after him, setting the house on fire and slaughtering its owners in front of Iyasco. When the militants turned on Iyasco, he and his four sons were separated from his wife, Benedictta, and their daughter.

'The man and boys were for the kill,' writes Mrs Gadazama. 'But the Lord stepped in and the leaders of that particular group of militants said women and children were not to be killed. This statement narrowly saved Shalom, the youngest son, who was just about to be hacked down. As he was pushed away, he was telling them about the love of the Lord Jesus Christ. This infuriated the militants more.'

Benedictta's abiding memory is of her husband being led away – still telling his attackers about the loving, saving grace of Jesus.

Benedictta took her children to the military barracks but realized that Shalom was missing. She went in search of her husband and son when the carnage was at its peak. Later, the next day, Shalom was found running among the dead. His father was slaughtered – his body, and the big Bible he was clinging to, were found in a gutter not very far from the church. The bodies of Iyasco and eight fellow believers were retrieved from a mass burial and Badarawa's Catholic priest gave them a Christian burial.

Local Christians ensured that Benedictta and her children were rehoused, but Benedictta says life is not the same. She misses her husband and cannot forget the sight of him being led away to be slaughtered: 'His message about the loving and saving grace of Jesus at his point of death are still very loud in her ears,' writes Mrs Gadazama.

Benedictta's hope is that Iyasco's martyrdom will cause many – including those who murdered him – to turn to Jesus as a result of this message of grace, and that her children will pick up their father's Bible, dust it off and follow in his footsteps.

Esther Jinkai Ethan (?–2003), Nigeria

Bishop Benjamin Kwashi also pays tribute to evangelist Esther Jinkai Ethan, who was stabbed to death on 8 June 2003 in the town of Numan in the state of Adamawa. The chief suspect, Muhammad Salisu, a Muslim water vendor, has never been brought to trial.

Mrs Ethan was stabbed after returning home from a session of street evangelism. Her children later countered media reports that their mother died as the result of an argument between her and Muhammad Salisu: 'We never heard our mother quarrelling with Muhammad Salisu,' said Benedict, the eldest of Mrs Ethan's four children. 'Our mother's killing was religiously motivated.'

Chapter 3

The price of faith under militant Islam

Murtala Marti Dangora (sentenced to death, 1980), Kano, Nigeria

The Revd Murtala Marti Dangora from Kano, northern Nigeria, began his Christian life 25 years ago with a baptism of fire. While many people in Nigeria become Christians without difficulties, Revd Dangora's decision to convert from Islam brought an instant death sentence from Muslim authorities, writes Obed Minchakpu, who reports from Jos for Compass News.

Revd Dangora has been detained, dragged to court, and publicly assaulted for becoming a Christian in April 1980 through the ministry of Haggai Latim, a missionary from the Evangelical Church of West Africa (ECWA).

'I was attracted to Christianity because of the love showed to me by the missionary,' Revd Dangora told Compass News. 'In Islam, anybody who is not a Muslim is to be despised. We did not deal with people who are not Muslims, so when the missionary tried preaching to me, I hated him.

'But the surprising thing is that this Christian missionary kept coming. He would always be around when something bad happened to me or my family. He was always there to encourage us. I was touched by his love towards me and my family. It was this act of love that moved me into resolving to become a Christian.'

Then the persecution started. The Muslim leaders of his native Dangora village, in the Kiru area of Kano State, ordered him arrested and brought before the community leader.

'I was interrogated as to why I got converted, and I was told that unless I renounced Christianity, I should be prepared to pay the price of leaving Islam – death,' he says. 'I was told

Roy Pontoh was 15 when he was
martyred in Ambon, Indonesia on
20 January 1999. *Photo: Open Doors*

'Jesus!' was the last word uttered by Roy Pontoh, before he was killed. He is
buried in this simple grave. *Photo: Open Doors*

Sister Maria Lourdes in East Timor with one of the children cared for by her community. Sister Lourdes' community fed 15,000 people from one barrel of rice for three weeks, while fighting in East Timor was at its worst: 'Each day I got up, I prayed, and then I started cooking rice,' she said. 'The day it ran out was the day the international peacekeepers came.'

Pastor Simon is pictured with a Burmese bombshell which has been cut into two and serves as the bell to summon people to church in the Thai–Burma borderlands. Instead of swords into ploughshares in Burma today may we have bombs into bells – and may these bells soon ring for peace and justice for all the people of Burma!

Rinaldy Damanik: released after serving two years and four months of his three-year sentence in Central Sulawesi, Indonesia. 'I would prefer to go to the scaffold for the truth than to accept freedom for a lie,' he said. *Photo: Compass Direct*

Allen Yuan, who was 91 when he died in August 2005, China. He spent a total of 21 years and eight months in prison because of his Christian faith. He is pictured with his wife Alice who cared for their six children during Allen's imprisonment. *Photo: Open Doors*

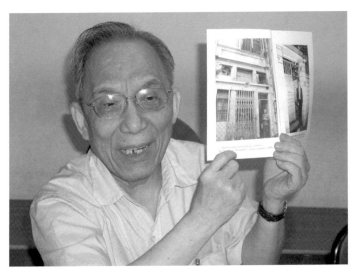

Born in 1924, Pastor Samuel Lamb has spent a quarter of his life in prison for his faith. He still preaches on Sundays in his large house church in Guangzhou, China. *Photo: Compass Direct*

Bishop Pargev Martirosyan, Primate of the Artsakh Diocese of the Armenian Apostolica Church. Although his home in Nagorno Karabakh received a direct hit from a large bomb, he still said: 'If we want God's victory, we must love. Even if there are demonic forces at work, not only in this conflict, but in other parts of the world, we must still love – we must always love.'

Alexander Men, a Russian Orthodox priest who was murdered on 9 September 1990; house-searches and interrogations were a feature of his life. *Photo source:* http://en.wikipedia.org/wiki/Image:FrAlexander Men.jpg

Benjamin Kwashi, Bishop of Jos, Nigeria, who says in the Foreword to this book: 'As we pray for those who are suffering persecution now, let us all flee from spiritual death by committing our lives to the Lord Jesus Christ, so that whenever and however physical death appears, we may be counted as faithful servants, called through his grace to enter the Kingdom of God.'

The funeral of Revd Bitrus Manjang, Victoria, his daughter-in-law who was pregnant, and Jessy, his grandson. They were killed on Thursday 12 December, 2002, when Fulani militia and Muslim fundamentalists attacked their home village of Rim, Plateau State, Nigeria.

Revd Bitrus Manjang, one-time Vice-President of the Church of Christ in Nigeria (COCIN).

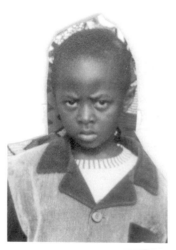

Revd Manjang's grandson Jessy, who died in the attack on Rim in December 2002.

Rev Murtala Marti Dangora from Kano, northern Nigeria, who has been detained, dragged to court, and publicly assaulted for becoming a Christian in April 1980. *Photo: Compass Direct*

Bishop Macram Gassis, the Roman Catholic Bishop for the Diocese of El Obeid in Sudan, exiled because he challenged the National Islamic Front regime which had seized power by military coup in 1989.

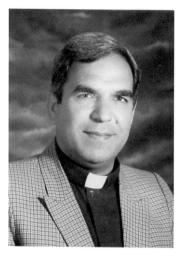

Assemblies of God minister, Hussein Soodmand, executed in December 1990 after an Iranian sharia court condemned him for apostasy. *Photo: Elam Ministries*

An outspoken campaigner for religious freedom in Iran, Bishop Haik Hovsepian-Mehr disappeared in January 1994. According to government officials, his body was found by the police in one of the suburbs of Tehran. He had been stabbed several times in the chest. His family were not notified until ten days later. *Photo: Elam Ministries*

After Bishop Haik's death, Tateos Michaelian succeeded him as chairman of Iran's Council of Protestant Ministers. Michaelian was last seen alive leaving his home in Tehran on 29 June 1994 in response to a telephone call. *Photo: Elam Ministries*

After spending nine years in an Iranian prison on the charge of apostasy, Mehdi Dibaj was tried in December 1993, found guilty and sentenced to death. Due to pressure from human rights groups, he was released in January 1994, but he was found murdered on 5 July 1994. *Photo: Elam Ministries* clearly that the Quran provides that any Muslim that abandons the faith must die.'

Muslim extremists have assaulted him, and Revd Dangora realizes he easily could have died by now. 'It is God that has kept me alive to this very moment,' he believes. 'I could have been killed and forgotten years ago. It has happened to others.'

Encouraged by Latim, who taught him the Bible, Revd Dangora did not return to Islam. After a year of growing in the Christian faith, Revd Dangora gave a plot of land he inherited from his father to Latim, so that a church could be built in Dangora village. This benevolence also earned him and Latim eight weeks of detention in a police cell. 'I was told by the police and council authorities that I had no right to donate my land to the church,' he says.

While in detention, the missionary encouraged him not to despair. 'At that time, I was only a year old in the Christian faith. I had just converted from Islam to Christianity,' Dangora says. Latim told him that persecution is part of the Christian life and to expect it.

'In detention, we sang Christian hymns, just like Paul and Silas did while in prison. The policemen, who were all Muslims, ordered us to shut up, but we ignored them and sang on joyfully.'

After an eight-week trial, the court in Kiru convicted them of building a church without government approval and ordered them to demolish it.

'Revd Inusa Ado was the chairman of the Kano district of ECWA at that time,' Revd Dangora says. 'The officials came to Kiru and explained that we committed no wrong in building a church sanctuary. But the police and the council officials insisted that we must apply and get approval from the government before we build a church in Kiru.' Revd Dangora did apply for approval. 'But as I am talking to you now, twenty-five years later, our application for the building of the church has not been granted,' he says. Hundreds of churches in Kano State face such difficulties, he adds.

Christian leaders in Kano liken their experiences under the Islamic regime to that of a people in captivity. They said Christians are being oppressed, discriminated against and humiliated because of their faith. In the past three years Revd Dangora has received notice of more than fifty cases of persecution of members of his church.

He also told Compass that Christian children in schools have no rights, especially during the fast of Ramadan. 'These children are not given food, as they are being forced to observe the Ramadan fast,' he explains. Children's Christian faith must be kept secret for them to be admitted into public schools in the first place. He explains: 'There is a lot of segregation here. The moment you are a Christian, your children are denied admission into public schools.'

Thus Christians in rural areas of Kano, he says, are afraid to send their children to public schools for fear that they will be forced to convert to Islam. 'Even in government schools, Christian children are being forced to become Muslims. They are being forced to study Arabic, Islam, and say Islamic prayers. They have no Christian teachers to teach them Christian religious knowledge.'

Moreover, he says, the government refuses to grant churches permission to establish schools in rural areas. For example, Christians in Bari Dorayi village built a nursery and primary school for their children, but the government stopped the building of the school.

'The strategy is to force Christians to send their children to public schools so that they can be forced to become Muslims,' Revd Dangora says. 'Sharia here is aimed at victimizing the Church. The first impression Muslim leaders gave was that sharia was purely meant to guide Muslims in the practice of their faith and that it would not affect Christians, but from the implementation of this religious law in Kano, we have come to realize that just as we expressed fears initially, it was specifically designed to strangulate Christianity.'

As Bishop Benjamin Kwashi explained in Chapter 1, the roots of the conflict in Nigeria are complex. Religion can be used as a pretext for fighting which, in reality, stems from economic, territorial or political motives. We include the following news briefs from Compass Direct to demonstrate the scale of violence which has led to the killing of Christians in Nigeria since the beginning of the millennium.

Twenty priests and pastors killed (February and May 2000), Kaduna, Nigeria

Twenty pastors from various church denominations were among the hundreds of Christians killed during the two religious crises that occurred in the northern Nigerian city of Kaduna in February and May 2000.

Among the pastors killed were Fr Clement Ozi Bello, 26, a Catholic priest; Revd Aniya Bobai of the ECWA; and Revd Bako Kabuk, along with Pastors Paul Chikira, David Maigari and Adamu Seko, of the Nigerian Baptist Convention.

Father Bello came from a Muslim family. His father is a Muslim, and his mother converted to Christianity shortly before the priest's ordination. Revd Bobai was killed in his church's pastorium. He was attacked by a Muslim mob and killed, and his church, the ECWA Unguwar Dosa, was set ablaze. The pastors of the Nigerian Baptist Convention were killed at the Kaduna campus of the Baptist Theological Seminary as they attempted to defend the school.

Christian preacher killed (August 2001), Abuja, Nigeria

Evangelist James Abdulkarim Yahaya, a popular Nigerian Christian preacher, was killed on 6 August 2001 by men suspected to be Muslim fundamentalists.

Yahaya was murdered in the Kado area of Abuja, Nigeria's capital city, when four well-armed men broke into his bedroom apartment and shot him as he slept. Yahaya was a former Muslim who converted to Christianity several years ago. He later became an itinerant preacher who travelled throughout

Nigeria. Christian leaders in Nigeria believe the preacher was killed as a result of his conversion from Islam to Christianity, because, under sharia, any convert from Islam must either recant or be killed.

Thirty Christians killed (August 2001), Bauchi State, Nigeria

At least thirty Christians were killed during an outbreak of violence between Muslims and Christians in areas of northern Nigeria's Bauchi State in August 2001. More than 158 Christian-owned houses were burned, along with two churches and a Bible school belonging to the Church of Christ in Nigeria. The religious clashes began after Bauchi Governor Alhaji Ahmed Adamu Muazu declared on 1 June 2001 that sharia applied to all persons in the state, not to Muslims only.

Fourteen worshippers killed (March 2002), Enugu, Nigeria

Fourteen Christians were killed in Enugu city in southeastern Nigeria on Thursday, 7 March 2002, when suspected government agents stormed a crusade ground in an alleged attempt to kill a Catholic priest who has been critical of government policies. The unidentified attackers released an unknown gas near the large crowd of worshippers at an all-night rally organized by the local Catholic church. The resulting stampede caused the deaths of fourteen worshippers and the hospitalization of hundreds of others. The fourteen worshippers who died at the crusade grounds were buried on 26 March after a requiem mass conducted by the Bishop of Enugu. He described the dead worshippers as 'martyrs'.

Five hundred die in religious conflict (July 2002), Wase, Nigeria

Some 500 people died in an outbreak of violence on 12 July 2002 between Muslims and Christians in Wase, a town in Plateau State in northern Nigeria. Prominent Christian leaders Vincent Lar, Gabriel Kumdum and Tsaih Bakinrijia, a former police chief, were among those killed in the tragedy. Solomon Lar, an adviser to Nigeria's president, said that more than ten Christian communities were ravaged and destroyed in the conflict. Some 10,000 people in these villages have been displaced and are now living as refugees. A canon of the Nigerian Anglican church blamed the attacks on a 'grudge' against Christians in this part of the country: 'We recognize the violence unleashed against church buildings, the holy men and the Taroh Christians generally in this light,' he said.

Police kill four Christians (December 2002), Enugu, Nigeria

On 14 December 2002, officers from the Nigeria federal police force killed four Catholic Christians and injured eight others as the group was returning home on a bus from a crusade and all-night prayer vigil. Charity Chukwu, 18, one of the passengers who managed to escape, said that police stopped the vehicle carrying the group to Enugu and demanded a bribe. 'The bus driver refused to offer the bribe because he was a Christian,' she said. '[The police] shot him point-blank and he died instantly.' When members of the group tried to calm the policemen, they were also shot dead. The rest fled on foot.

Two Catholic priests assassinated (August 2003), Awka, Nigeria

Two priests of the Roman Catholic church were assassinated in south-eastern Nigeria. According to a statement issued by the Roman Catholic Secretariat of the Nigerian Catholic Church in Lagos, Father Patrick Ekwuno of Awka diocese was killed in early August by three armed assassins at the mission house where he lived. Ekwuno was involved with the Catholic Church's Justice, Peace and Development programme. Father Vincent de Paul Nnabuife of Orlu diocese was killed later in the month. The statement of the Secretariat did not give the exact date of the murder. Over the years, several priests have been harassed because of their stand on religious liberty and human rights issues in the country.

Deaths of at least 350 people (February–April 2004), Plateau State, Nigeria

Fresh religious violence erupted in Yelwa town in Plateau State two months after Muslim militants killed a pastor and forty-eight members of his church there on 23 February 2004. The latest Muslim–Christian clash has resulted in the deaths of at least 350 people. Some press reports put the death toll as high as 630. According to police reports, 250 women and children are missing.

Christian student murdered (December 2004), Bauchi State, Nigeria

The Abubakar Tafawa Balewa University (ATBU) in Bauchi State was closed after Muslims attacked Christians in December 2004, resulting in the brutal murder of Sunday Nache Achi, an evangelical student leader on the ATBU campus. Five other

Christians were expelled for conducting an evangelistic outreach.

Christian woman shot dead (January 2005), Numan, Nigeria

On 28 January 2005, a Christian woman was shot dead by soldiers deployed to the town of Numan to keep order. Christian leaders told Compass News that the killing, combined with the state government's ousting of Numan's Christian monarch and its failure to prosecute the Muslim fanatic who killed Esther Jinkai Ethan in the town nineteen months before, amounts to persecution.

Two Christian youths killed (February 2005), Numan, Nigeria

Tensions escalated sharply between the Christian community of Numan, and government security forces deployed to keep peace between Muslims and Christians following the shooting deaths of two Christian young people. Police killed Ezekiel Eli and Kingsley Zadok Imburu on 7 February when the two joined a group opposing the arrest of a local Christian woman. Thirty Christian residents, including the Revd Nelson Malau, a pastor of the Lutheran Church of Christ in Nigeria, were arrested during the incident and were to stand trial in the Adamawa State capital.

Chapter 4
Sudan – cathedral under a tamarind tree

More than twenty years ago, my son Jonathan, a medical missionary at the time, told me of the acute shortage of nurses in Sudan. People were dying by the thousands of treatable diseases and famine. I believe that if God opens a door one should go through it. I am a qualified nurse, so I responded and spent several months in Sudan.

Since then I have been back twenty-eight times. Walking through the killing fields of victims of militant jihad, I have seen the impact of the jihad warriors' scorched-earth policy.

One particular visit to Bahr-el-Gazal is burned into my memory as my worst experience in terms of the sheer scale of the horror. Just a few days before I visited, the National Islamic Front regime's forces had swept through the area, slaughtering civilians and burning villages. It was sheer carnage – human bodies, cattle corpses, burned homes.

I will never forget the words of one Roman Catholic catechist, Santino Ring. His brother and brother-in-law had been killed and his sister had been captured as a slave. His church had been attacked, Bibles burned, crops destroyed. He told me that while the Sudanese regime spent one million dollars a day on the war, the Christians had nothing. 'Worse than that,' he said, 'we feel completely on our own. You're the only Christians who have even visited us for years.'

Then came the words which turned a knife in my heart. He asked: 'Doesn't the Church want us any more?' I sat under a tree and wept. What a challenge to the Church in the West! I want Santino to know that not only do we 'want' him, but we cherish him. And if the day must come when he will have to endure martyrdom, as so many already have, then we will try to be worthy of the price they are paying for our faith.

On several visits to Sudan I have travelled with Bishop Macram Gassis, whose stand against the regime led to his exile.

Macram Gassis (b. 1938), Sudan

Bishop Macram, the Roman Catholic bishop for the Diocese of El Obeid in Sudan, was exiled because he challenged the National Islamic Front (NIF) regime, which had seized power by military coup in 1989. This Islamist regime had declared military jihad against all who opposed it. The regime's victims included many Muslims as well as Christians and traditional believers.

The weapons of the jihad were threefold and formidable: military offensives against innocent civilians; the manipulation of aid; and slavery.

During the many years of bitter fighting, from the earliest days of the regime's rule to the eventual signing of a peace agreement in January 2005, it would carry out massive military offensives with its own army, combined with the Islamic jihad warriors, in areas which it simultaneously declared 'no go' to the United Nations Operation Lifeline Sudan and all the aid organizations working under the UN umbrella. Thus, no one could take aid to the victims or obtain evidence to tell the world of the atrocities the regime was perpetrating.

But there were always a few deviant individuals who would continue to try to reach the 'no go' areas to take aid to the people suffering there and to obtain evidence of the regime's systematic violations of human rights in those killing fields.

In my twenty-eight visits to Sudan in those bitter days, I witnessed the full horrors of the regime's jihad: huge swathes of land devastated by carnage and scorched-earth policy; innocent civilians – men, women and children – dying of disease and starvation in areas cut off from aid organizations; and the heartbreak of systematic slavery, especially in the borderlands between north and south Sudan.

Access to the 'no go' areas was illegal in the eyes of the NIF regime. Those who went did so at risk of being shot out of the sky or bombed on the ground. The regime also, I am told, gave me a five-year prison sentence in my absence for 'illegal entry'. However, it is part of a Christian mandate to try to be with the most outcast, forgotten and suffering people – and certainly the victims of full-scale military offensives in those parts of Sudan, designated 'no go' to major aid organizations, must have been among the most acutely suffering and deprived people on the earth at that time.

On some of my visits, I had the great privilege of travelling with Bishop Macram Gassis, who constantly risked his life to be with his people in those terrible days. I will never forget how the people loved him as he came to share their darkness, to bring practical help and spiritual ministry. One day is indelibly etched on my mind. We had arrived at a location which had recently suffered from military attacks by government soldiers and jihad warriors. Everything had been destroyed; many people killed; others captured and taken away as slaves. The survivors were destitute and shattered by the fate which had befallen them.

Forlorn, desperate, they gathered for Mass in what they called their 'cathedral under a tamarind tree'. Tamarind trees have branches which rise up and then sweep down to the ground, forming a natural shelter. Inside, the people had placed a few logs as benches – and that was their 'cathedral'. The bishop preached his sermon and his words spoke directly to their most painful, sensitive points of need:

Here we are, in this most beautiful cathedral – not made by human hands, but by nature and by God. And it is filled with the people of God, and especially with children.

You people here in Sudan still smile, in spite of suffering persecution and slavery. Your smiles put us to shame. Many of you are suffering from slavery, but remember, if that happens to you, or someone whom you love, there is no need to be ashamed, as you are not a real slave. You are children of a God who has said we can call him 'Abba, Father' – so you are children of God, of liberty and truth.

But slavery is a terrible thing. If it happens to you, remember it is not you who are the real slave, but those who do cruel and terrible things – they are slaves to sin.

Many of you are embarrassed because you are naked. Do not be embarrassed! Yours is not true nakedness. True nakedness is to be without love. Be clothed in love – that is Christianity – and show your love to those who do not know our Lord of Love.

We must leave you. But we will not forget you. We will remember you as those who are especially close to Christ, because every day you are taking up your cross and walking with Him on the road to Calvary.

We will pray for you. But prayer without deeds is dead, as love without action is dead. Our prayer and our love must be in action for you.

I came, I saw, I heard, I touched – and I am enriched.

All who have been with the persecuted church can identify with those final words: we all return enriched, receiving immeasurably more than we can ever give.

Bishop Macram was ordained in 1964 and appointed Apostolic Administrator of El Obeid in 1983, becoming bishop in 1988. The 21-year-long conflict in his country will link for ever the words 'Darfur', 'Janjaweed' and 'genocide'. The war was sparked by government efforts to impose Islamic law on the mostly Christian south in 1983, and was fuelled by the NIF regime's determination to control access to the south's rich oil reserves. An estimated two million people, many of them children, died as a result of the war – before the horrors of the massacres in Darfur began to reach our TV screens.

In his Christmas address in 1998, Bishop Macram read this powerful message from the children of Sudan:

My name is Rafi, from the Nuba mountains, and my friend is Mabior from Abyei.

Both of us are Sudanese children.

Both of us are nine years old.

We have a message for you this Christmas. Please listen . . . meditate . . . and act.

We children do not harbour hatred and discrimination, adults instil it in us.

We do not cultivate intolerance and fanaticism, adults do it.

We do not enslave, rape, and declare holy war, adults practise it.

We do not make guns, bombs, and tanks for war, adults manufacture it.

We do not wage war, kill, torture, and assassinate, it is the doing of adults.

We do not plant land mines and drop cluster bombs to maim innocent children, it is the action of adults.

We do not use food as a weapon, it is the policy of adults.

The adults are the source of our tragedy and of our suffering.

The adults are the cause of our agony, extermination and death.

We are annihilated by man-made famine; thousands of us children have died, and others are just moving skeletons.

We are killed by disease, we are terrorised by aerial bombardment.

We are orphans and refugees, we are deprived of clean water, and we are robbed of our dignity as human beings.

Adults call us the future of the church and of society . . . Do they really mean it?

We have no voice in the world of adults, we have no say and we have no power.

We are simple and we are innocent. We are the special friends of JESUS.

He listens to our sorrows and sees our tears. We are the new children of Bethlehem.

We have no adequate words to express our gratitude to those who saved us.

Many came to our rescue. We plead with others to do the same.

We are the future of the church and of society.

Do not be indifferent.

Do not be silent.

SILENCE KILLS US.

Please care and share because it is Christmas.

It is the feast of the child Jesus, it is the feast of the children.[1]

Josephine Bakhita (1869–1947), Sudan

A one-time slave, Josephine Bakhita is now a symbol of faith and unity for suffering Sudan.

Josephine was born in the region of Darfur in 1869. She was kidnapped and enslaved by Arab traders when she was a child. Her captors gave her the name Bakhita, which means 'fortunate'. She was bought and sold five times, until 1882, when she was purchased by Calisto Legnani, an Italian consular agent who took her to Italy.

There, she heard about Christianity, and was baptized in 1890. Three years later, she entered the Congregation of the Cannosiana Religious, and lived in a convent in Schio, Vicenza, in northern Italy, where she carried out the most menial tasks, and very quickly gained a reputation for sanctity. When she died on 8 February 1947, a long line of mourners filed past her coffin for several days. She was canonized by Pope John Paul II on 1 October 2000 – Sudan's first canonized saint.

Chapter 5

Uganda – an African crucible

Uganda has its own stories of genocide. The country still honours the twenty-six Christians who were martyred at Namugongo on 3 June 1886, at the climax of a campaign against those who converted to Christianity from tribal religions. But, rather than deterring the growth of Christianity, the martyrdom of these early believers seems to have sparked its growth.

In the nineteenth century Arabs and Europeans arrived in the kingdoms which became modern Uganda and the country was ruled as a British protectorate from 1894 until it achieved independence in 1962. The first prime minister, Milton Obote, declared himself president in 1966, ushering in decades of coups and counter-coups. Idi Amin took power in 1971 and his dictatorial regime was responsible for 300,000 deaths. Under his rule anyone suspected of dissent was arrested; many were killed. Hundreds of soldiers from the Lango and Acholi tribes were shot and killed in their barracks. Uganda's Asian population of about 80,000 people was expelled.

During Amin's reign of terror, many Christians were killed for alleged offences. For example, a preacher reading a psalm which mentioned Israel on a radio programme was shot for the 'offence' in 1972. The editor of Uganda's Roman Catholic newspaper, who criticized Amin, died 'in a car accident'. When a post-mortem revealed that he had been shot and strangled before the car was set alight, the doctor who had conducted the post-mortem 'disappeared'. The new editor of the newspaper was arrested and, six weeks later, was said to have died in prison.

In 1973 Bishop Festo Kivengere met with Idi Amin to voice his opposition to the killing of three men from his diocese by a government firing squad on a trumped-up charge. In *African*

An African crucible

Saints: Saints, Martyrs, and Holy People from the Continent of Africa, Frederick Quinn quotes the bishop's description of the execution:

February 10 began as a sad day for us in Kabale. People were commanded to come to the stadium and witness the execution. Death permeated the atmosphere. A silent crowd of about three thousand was there ready to watch. I had permission from the authorities to speak to the men before they died, and two of my fellow ministers were with me. They brought the men in a truck and unloaded them. They were handcuffed and their feet were chained. The firing squad stood at attention. As we walked into the center of the stadium, I was wondering what to say. How do you give the Gospel to doomed men who are probably seething with rage?

We approached them from behind, and as they turned to look at us, what a sight! Their faces were all alight with an unmistakable glow and radiance. Before we could say anything, one of them burst out: 'Bishop, thank you for coming! I wanted to tell you. The day I was arrested, in my prison cell, I asked the Lord Jesus to come into my heart. He came in and forgave me all my sins! Heaven is now open, and there is nothing between me and my God! Please tell my wife and children that I am going to be with Jesus. Ask them to accept him into their lives as I did.' The other two men told similar stories, excitedly raising their hands, which rattled their handcuffs.

I felt that what I needed to do was to talk to the soldiers, not to the condemned. So I translated what the men had said into a language the soldiers understood. The military men were standing there with guns cocked and bewilderment on their faces. They were so dumbfounded that they forgot to put the hoods over the men's faces! The three faced the firing squad standing close together. They looked toward the people and began to wave, handcuffs and all. The people waved back. Then shots were fired . . .[1]

Janani Luwum (1922–1977), Uganda

Archbishop Janani Luwum incurred Idi Amin's wrath because he helped Christians who were suffering under Amin's reign of terror. But Janani refused to hate Amin: 'We must love the president. We must pray for him. He is a child of God,' he told the people. But the archbishop was outspoken in his condemnation of the bloodletting: massacres which included the killing of the entire population of Milton Obote's home village in February 1977.

Amin chose to interpret the archbishop's calls for peace as a threat. He condemned church leaders for 'preaching revolution' and, on 5 February 1977, he had the archbishop's home raided in search of weapons. Three days later the archbishop met with his fellow bishops and drafted a letter to the president, asking to see him to discuss the country's welfare. Janani knew the risk he was taking but said, 'Even if he [Amin] kills me, my blood will save the nation.'

Amin took his opportunity to strike. He accused the archbishop of treason and brought Janani to trial on 16 February 1977, together with six fellow bishops. A large cache of arms was displayed as 'evidence'.

In *Candles in the Dark*, journalist and broadcaster Mary Craig reported on what happened next:

> Janani shook his head in silent denial.
>
> 'They intend to kill me, but I am not afraid,' he whispered to Bishop Festo.
>
> 'What shall we do with the traitors?' shouted the Vice President, who was in charge of the 'trial'. The scene was so reminiscent of a trial that took place some 2,000 years earlier in front of Pontius Pilate that it might almost have been stage managed.
>
> 'Kill them, kill them,' screamed the soldiers [there were 3,000 on parade at the trial].
>
> 'Put up your hands, those who want them shot in public,'

demanded the Vice President, and a forest of hands rose into the air, without a single dissenter.

But in front of such a distinguished gathering, this was no time for allowing lynching law. The semblance of civilised behaviour must be preserved. The bishops were merely ordered into a side room . . . As they sat there, an official told Archbishop Luwum that the President wanted to see him in the next room. Janani rose to his feet and smiled at Bishop Festo. 'There is something I have not told you,' he said. 'Three days ago a girl came to warn me that I was number one on the Security Forces' death list. She overheard some of the men talking in Swahili about it. She wanted me to escape, but I told her: I cannot. I am the Archbishop. I must stay.'

It was his farewell. Saying, 'I can see the hand of the Lord in this,' he turned away from his friend and walked calmly through the door . . .[2]

Janani Luwum was not seen alive again.

That evening, Radio Uganda announced that he had been arrested. The next morning a further announcement said that he had died 'in a motor accident'. Bishop Festo, who went to the hospital to claim the body for burial, said, 'We have talked to eye witnesses who claim that they saw him shot, and with others who saw the bodies in the morgue with bullet wounds.'[3]

The Americas V

Chapter 1

Killed in action

Choice is the touchstone of true martyrdom and separates martyrs from victims.

Diana Dewar[1]

Dora Tenenoff's father, Richard, was taken hostage by guerilla fighters on the Panama–Colombia border in 1993 with fellow American missionaries David Mankins and Mark Rich. The men, who were part of the New Tribes Mission, were taken hostage by Revolutionary Armed Forces of Colombia (FARC) guerillas. Their bodies have never been found. While the families waited for news, Dora wrote this poem; she was 15 at the time.

There once was a man . . .

There once was a man, a man I once knew.
Who told me stories every night, laughed at my jokes, and
held me tight.
He told me, 'Don't quit! Always fight the good fight!'
He said, 'Love the Lord with all your heart,
and serve Him with all your might!'
He begged me, 'Do right!

There once was a man, a man I once knew.
Who taught me how to tie my shoe,
and gently smiled at every picture that I drew.
He told me, 'When you start something, don't stop until the
job is through.'
He said, 'I love you.'

There once was a man, a man I once knew.
I saw him in my dream, and it made me scream,
I called out, 'Daddy!'
but he told me nothing,

Killed in action

He had nothing to say.
For what can you say,
When you are far, so very far away?
'Daddy?' I said,
then a voice echoed in my head.
I lay quiet and still in my bed.
Again the voice,
'Your daddy made a choice,
a choice to serve Me with all his might,
To not give up,
to fight the good fight!
He is doing a job for me and is not yet through,
so remember: I love you!'

There now is a man, a man I now know.
He lived and He died to save men from their sin.
He made it possible for us to be born again.
I know because my daddy told me so.
And even though he's no longer here,
My God will always be near
To fill in the gaps and show me which way to go.
I miss my dad so much,
But God has a plan.
So for now I'll just wait and watch the work of His Hand.

There once was a man,
A man I once knew.
He's now just a memory slowly fading away.
'Dead or Alive?' you ask.
'I don't know,' I say.
So I beg you, Please Pray!!
Pray my daddy knows that every night,
I whisper, 'Daddy, I love you!'

There now is a man, a man I now know.
Every day He becomes more real to me.
Every day in Him, I grow.
Every day I pray that my love for Him will show
I've made a choice, to serve Him with all my might.
To not give up, to fight the good fight.

Here on earth, I may not see my dad again,
but that's all right.
'Cause when my life is through,
I'll finally hear them both say
My child, I love you!![2]

I heard this moving poem for the first time at a Christian
Solidarity Worldwide conference. It is a poignant reminder of
the pain a martyr leaves behind and the cost which their families must continue to bear.

In compiling this book we have had to be selective. There
are so many more stories which deserve to be told, among
them numerous accounts of missionaries who have lost their
lives taking Christianity to countries other than their own.

Although I travel frequently to the United States, I have had
little personal contact with Christians suffering persecution in
North or South America; hence this section is short. I recognize the sacrifice made by Christians from North America as
they encourage and support Christians around the world.
Many, such as Richard Tenenoff, David Mankins and Mark
Rich, have paid the ultimate price. By telling their story, we
also pay tribute to hundreds more missionaries who have died.

Richard Tenenoff, David Mankins and Mark Rich (taken hostage, 1993), Panama

Rick Tenenoff, Dave Mankins, Mark Rich and their families
lived in the village of Púcuro in the Darien region of Panama.
Púcuro is a village of approximately 300 Kuna people, in the
south-eastern part of the country, about fifteen miles from the
Colombian border.

The missionaries, from New Tribes Mission (NTM) in the
USA, were in Panama at the invitation of the leaders of the village. In addition to studying the Kuna language and culture,
the missionaries were involved in linguistic analysis, teaching
the people to read and write in their own language, and admin-
istering medical assistance.

According to a detailed report by NTM, on 31 January 1993, armed guerrillas burst into the missionaries' home. They held Rick, Dave and Mark at gunpoint while their wives packed a few belongings. Patti Tenenoff, Nancy Mankins and Tania Rich last saw their husbands, hands bound behind their backs, marching into the Panamanian jungle.

The women returned to the USA, but their husbands were never seen by their families again. Two-way radio contact with the guerrillas brought demands, threats and deadlines. Just before Christmas 1993, the kidnappers proved their hostages were still alive by allowing Dave, Mark and Rick's voices to be heard on the radio. But, in January 1994, following routine radio contact, guerrilla communication unexpectedly ceased.

In subsequent months, NTM sought the aid of humanitarian organizations, the US, Colombian and other Latin American governments, and the news media. The NTM Crisis Team followed countless leads. They gathered reports of sightings of the men in captivity, their activities and movements. NTM also met with guerilla agents to appeal for the humanitarian release of the men.

In September 2001 members of NTM's Crisis Committee and the three wives agreed that, given the available evidence, it was time to assume that the men were dead.

Rick Tenenoff was born in Los Angeles, California, on 23 September 1956. He and his wife, Patti, went to Panama in 1986. A year and a half later, they began a ministry with the Kuna people in the village of Púcuro. Rick was studying the Kuna language and culture and was compiling a Kuna dictionary.

Dave Mankins was born in Susanville, California, on 16 March 1949. He and his wife, Nancy, began serving with NTM in Panama in 1984, and in 1986 moved to the village of Púcuro to work with the Kuna people. Dave translated the Bible lessons into the Kuna language.

Mark Rich was born on 5 September 1969, in Mollendo, Peru. He and his wife, Tania, arrived in Panama in 1991, and moved to Púcuro in August 1992 to begin language and culture study.

Missionaries like Rick, Dave and Mark have died in 'active service'. They believed they were fulfilling a calling from

Christ to 'go into all the world'. Christians in every country owe a deep debt of gratitude to those who have responded to Christ's commission – as three generations of the Saune family in Peru can testify.

Justiniano Saune (1904–1989), Romulo Saune (?–?) and Ruben Saune (?–?), Peru

Missionaries from the United States introduced Justiniano Saune to Christianity. His grandson, Joshua Saune, the third generation of Christians in the family, described his martyrdom to Dan Wooding of Assist News:

'One Sunday, standing before his people, he told them, "This is the last Sunday that I am before you. Next Sunday, I'm not going to be here, because the Lord has called me home."'

'The next day, he was pulled from his house. Many times before, the Lord had warned him to escape as Shining Path were coming to kill him, and he did escape. But, now the Lord told him, "This time they are coming to take your life, and you're coming home with me."'

The Communist Party of Peru (PCP) is often referred to as 'Shining Path' by the media. Shining Path (Sendero Luminoso) is a Maoist guerilla movement, which has been responsible for the deaths of 100,000 people in Peru, including many Quechua Indians.

Joshua continues: 'The Shining Path got him, and they were going to ask him questions about his faith. For them, the Gospel is a wall that must come down. Since my grandfather told them that the solution for our country is found in Jesus Christ, they started to kill him right there. He was killed in a horrendous way. His eyes were taken out, his tongue was cut out and his heart pulled out while he was still alive. That's how he died at the age of 85 years, defending the Gospel of Jesus Christ.'

According to the Peruvian government, 800 pastors in Peru and close to 30,000 Christian men, women and children have been killed. Entire congregations have been murdered.

Several other members of Joshua's family have also died at

the hands of Shining Path guerillas, including his brothers Romulo and Ruben Saune and three of his nephews. Joshua explains what happened.

> They had been working in Peru among my people and they had travelled to the mountains of Ayacucho to take the Gospel and fellowship to the people, because then, the Quechua Christians were in despair, living in caves, with no food, just hiding from the guerillas. My brothers knew that they had to do something for them. They decided to fellowship with them and show them that our great God really wanted to take care of them.
>
> However, when Romulo, Ruben and my other relatives were coming back from the mountains they were killed. There was an ambush set up on the road they were returning home on, and they were shot by Shining Path guerillas. My mother and father were with them; my brothers and three of my nephews died two yards away from them.

Joshua, now president of the Quechua Church, which has more than 200 indigenous churches in its fellowship, adds: 'Altogether, approximately 100,000 people have been killed in Peru, because of these atrocities . . . I myself have lost half of my family, because we chose to follow Christ.'

Following Christ, and speaking out against poverty and injustice, has cost some Christians everything. Oscar Romero is one of South America's Christians who paid that ultimate price.

Oscar Romero (1917–1980), El Salvador

'I have often been threatened with death,' Archbishop Oscar Romero told a Guatemalan reporter two weeks before his assassination. 'If they kill me, I shall arise in the Salvadoran people. If the threats come to be fulfilled, from this moment I offer my blood to God for the redemption and resurrection of El Salvador. Let my blood be a seed of freedom and the sign that hope will soon be reality.'

On 24 March 1980, Oscar Romero was celebrating Mass at a small chapel near his cathedral in San Salvador, when he was killed by a gunman. As he lay dying, his last words are said to have been: 'May God have mercy on the assassins.'

Because of his outspoken political activism and theology, the archbishop was not popular with the political establishment or the Church hierarchy. His ministry on behalf of the poor won him no friends among El Salvador's wealthy elite. A prophet of justice and a peacemaker, he made enemies in the armed forces and the death squads who tortured, raped and murdered anyone who opposed the system.

Romero knew his outspokenness might lead to his death. He told one reporter: 'You can tell the people that if they succeed in killing me, that I forgive and bless those who do it. Hopefully, they will realize they are wasting their time. A bishop will die, but the Church of God, which is the people, will never perish.'

Describing the importance of Romero's Christ-like example to the people of El Salvador, Jesuit theologian Jon Sobrino said:

> To try to follow Monseñor Romero was to follow Jesus today
> in El Salvador . . . Monseñor is well used when our memory
> of him promotes all that has to do with hope, courage, and
> commitment. When the Salvadoran people work for peace,
> justice and reconciliation and are motivated by a belief in the
> God of the poor, they are following the example of Monseñor
> Romero who himself followed the crucified Christ and gave
> himself to the poor of his time.[3]

Although he lived with the imminent prospect of death, his message was full of hope. On 17 December 1978 he said:

> The Christian, the Christian community, must not despair.
> If someone dies in the family, we must not weep like people
> without hope. If the skies have darkened in our nation's
> history, let us not lose hope. We are a community of hope,
> and like the Israelites in Babylon, let us hope for the hour of
> liberation. It will come. It will come because God is faithful,
> says St. Paul. This joy must be like a prayer. "He who called
> you is faithful," and He will keep His promises.[4]

The
Middle East

VI

Chapter 1

Saudi Arabia – reviled, persecuted . . . blessed

Blessed are you when people revile you and persecute you and
utter all kinds of evil against you falsely on my account.
Rejoice and be glad, for your reward is great in heaven, for in
the same way they persecuted the prophets who were before
you.

(Matthew 5:11–12, New Revised Standard Version)

The Arab world – which includes the Middle East – stretches
from the Atlantic to the Indian Ocean. Most Arabs are Muslims, although there are an estimated 14 million Christian Arabs
living in communities in Egypt, Lebanon, Syria, Iraq, Jordan,
Israel and Palestine.

In the Middle East, Israel stands out as the crucible of world
religions. Its population is just seven million: of every hundred
people, seventy-five are Jewish, sixteen are Muslim and two are
Christians.

Israel is surrounded by the Arab world's 300 million, mainly
Muslim people. The vast majority of Muslims are peaceable,
law-abiding and often extremely hospitable, but there has been
a serious growth of militant Islam and, unless we take militant
Islam seriously, there will be a backlash against all Muslims, as
militant Islam is associated with acts of terror, terror creates fear,
and fear tends to blur distinctions, prompting indiscriminate
and possibly violent reaction.

Islam makes no distinction between secular and religious life.
Hence Islamic law or sharia is applied to every aspect of life
from banking and dress codes to worship and legal deterrents.
The implementation of sharia in the Muslim world is associated
with policies which are fundamentally incompatible with the
Universal Declaration of Human Rights in several key dimen-

sions, for example, the freedom to choose and change religion:
Islam is basically a one-way street – you can choose to become
a Muslim, but then if you want to change, you will commit
apostasy, which may well bring death. Also, sharia does not
admit equality before the law between men and women or
between Muslims and non-Muslims.[1]

Islam's two holiest places – Mecca and Medina – are in Saudi
Arabia, which is a monarchy governed according to sharia law.
According to Open Doors, which monitors the persecuted
Church,

> The Church in Saudi Arabia is living under the most difficult
> circumstances. The regime has declared the entire Arabian
> peninsula 'haram', forbidden to all other religions, and it is
> enforcing this prohibition strictly.
>
> The Saudi religious police (Mutawwa'in) are practically
> omnipresent in Saudi Arabia. Their power is almost limitless.
> The Mutawwa'in have special prisons where they torture their
> victims. Their aim is to ascertain that all citizens (and expatri-
> ates) adhere to strict Islamic legislation.
>
> The religious police see it as their main task to track down
> believers of other religions and to prevent gatherings of these
> believers. For this reason they have constructed a wide net-
> work of informers. Meetings of Christians therefore have to
> take place in the deepest form of secrecy. It is also one of the
> reasons why expatriate Christians are reluctant to admit Saudi
> nationals to their meetings.
>
> Meetings of Christians can only take place informally at
> embassy compounds or in people's homes. These secret
> gatherings are hunted down with increasing diligence and the
> leaders subjected to humiliating beatings, imprisonment and
> expulsion from the country.

I have had little personal contact with Christians in Middle
Eastern countries so I am grateful to Open Doors, Compass
Direct, Elam Ministries and other news sources for allowing us
to record the stories of these modern saints and martyrs,
enabling us to pay tribute to their perseverance under severe
persecution.

Wally Magdangal (death sentence, 1992), Saudi Arabia

Pastor Wally Magdangal was one Christian in Saudi Arabia whose activities fell foul of sharia. A Filipino Christian, he led a secret house church in Riyadh during the Gulf War. But the growing church became too noticeable and Magdangal was arrested. He was sentenced to death by public hanging on 25 December 1992 for blaspheming Islam.

In an interview with Jeff Sellers of *Christianity Today* Magdangal said his interrogators demanded the names of other Christians he knew. He refused.

'Eventually I was so weak, they placed the pad of paper in my lap, and they forced the pencil into my hand. I was weeping, and I said, "Lord, you've got to help me here," and I began to write the names of Billy Graham, Charles Spurgeon, and others. After a few days, they were so mad, because they'd been all over Saudi Arabia looking for those people.'[2]

Magdangal was kept in solitary confinement, interrogated many times and tortured. On the day he was due to be hanged, the prison commander arrived with orders to deport him. The appeals to the monarchy of Saudi Arabia from his wife, daughter, human rights organizations and Christians from all over the world had been effective.

Ruel Janda and Arnel Beltran (beheaded, 1997), Saudi Arabia

Two Filipino Catholics involved in Bible studies and Christian prayers in a Saudi prison were beheaded on 4 May 1997.

Barbara Baker of Compass Direct reported that the men were convicted and executed in Riyadh for 'forced armed robbery'. They had been accused of striking a Riyadh shop employee on the head with an iron bar. However, Donato Lama, a former cellmate of the executed men, said they had been imprisoned on 'false and fabricated' charges.

'There had been an argument at the store where they worked,' Lama said, 'and a fight broke out between them and some Pakistani and Egyptian nationals. Afterwards, they took revenge against Ruel and Arnel by accusing them of stealing from the store.'

Lama was confined in Al-Malaz Prison with Janda and Beltran until his release in March 1997. He believed they were executed because they had been conducting Bible studies and praying with other prisoners.

The two executed men had been in prison since 7 April 1995. Muslim Filipino cellmates reported them to guards for their Christian activities.

Donato Lama (seventy lashes, 1997), Saudi Arabia

Roman Catholic lay worker Donato Lama was arrested in November 1995, according to Open Doors. The Muttawwa'in raided his house and discovered some photographs of Lama leading a prayer meeting.

Amnesty International reported that Lama was shackled and handcuffed as well as beaten while under interrogation during two weeks' incommunicado detention. During his trial he was forced to stand in front of the judge with his legs chained and wearing handcuffs. He was sentenced to 18 months' imprisonment and seventy lashes. He described how restraints were frequently used on those in prison: 'They would handcuff your hands and hang them on a post [and] you would have to stand for two to five hours . . . When our embassy officials would come and visit us . . . they would handcuff us and shackle also our legs . . . Sometimes it would hurt your legs with bruising. Sometimes the guard would drag you; it would be very hard to walk.'

Donato Lama was finally released and deported in March 1997.

Rene Camahort (deported, 1998), Saudi Arabia

Filipino Rene Camahort became a Christian while he was jailed in Al-Malaz Prison's Section Four, a large cell housing 80–100 Filipinos and other Asians.

Barbara Baker of Compass Direct reported: 'Christian believers managed to meet inconspicuously in small groups five times a day, while the Muslim inmates were praying in a far corner of the large cell.' Camahort joined a small group which met to pray, share Scripture verses and encourage one another.

When the key leader of the Bible studies, Donato Lama, was finally released and deported, Camahort took over leading the group but, Compass Direct reported, 'Prison authorities in desperation "exiled" Camahort from the other Filipinos in Section Four, transferring him into a cell of primarily Muslim, non-English-speaking prisoners'.

Officials continued to offer him early release and multiple benefits, from money to beautiful wives, if he would convert to Islam, Compass said. Not only did he refuse, but, according to a friend who visited Camahort in June 1998, at least three of his cellmates had become Christians through his witness.

He was deported in August 1998 after spending three years and nine months in the Riyadh jail.

Chapter 2
Iraq – past affliction and uncertain future

Since the end of the Iraq war, sectarian violence has prompted many Christians to flee Iraq, reports Open Doors USA. A wave of church bombings in August 2004 sent 30,000 or more Christians to neighbouring Syria and Jordan in search of refuge. According to most estimates, the Christian community in Iraq numbered between 550,000 to 600,000 at the time of the overthrow of Saddam Hussein in 2003.

The role of Islam in the Iraqi constitution is a deep concern for all Iraqi Christians. While the Kurds pushed for a secular constitution, the Shi'ites preferred that Islam be named the 'only source' of Iraqi legislation. In the new Iraqi constitution, ratified on 15 October 2005, Islam is the national religion and a basic foundation for the country's laws; however, freedom of religion is upheld. The preamble to the constitution states:

> We the people of Iraq, newly arisen from our disasters and looking with confidence to the future through a democratic, federal, republican system, are determined – men and women, old and young – to respect the rule of law, reject the policy of aggression, pay attention to women and their rights, the elderly and their cares, the children and their affairs, spread the culture of diversity and defuse terrorism.[1]

The first chapter states:

> Islam is the official religion and is a basic source of legislation:
>
> (a) No law can be passed that contradicts the undisputed rules of Islam.

(b) No law can be passed that contradicts the principles of democracy.

(c) No law can be passed that contradicts the rights and basic freedoms outlined in this constitution.

This constitution guarantees the Islamic identity of the majority of the Iraqi people and full religious rights for all individuals and the freedom of creed and religious practices.[2]

According to Open Doors, Christians fear that the role of Islam could lead to religious clerics dictating Iraqi law, along with a diminishing role for Christians at all levels of government.

The Chaldean Archbishop of Kirkuk, Louis Sako, told Open Doors: 'We feel as Christians [that] we are isolated as a minority.' Archbishop Sako, who moved to Kirkuk in 2004, appealed to the Christian world: 'We need solidarity. We ask you to help the Islamic countries to respect human rights and values, to respect human persons as absolute value [before] God.'

Maher Dahkel, Firas, Imaam Raheem and Yeheya (missing, September 2005), Baghdad, Iraq

At the time of writing, the beginning of 2006, Iraq is still news. But one story, which failed to achieve headlines in the western media, demonstrates how conflict in Iraq is affecting Christians. Among the many abductions, suicide bombings and assassinations, four Christians have gone missing. No ransom demand has been received, and there is increasing evidence to suggest that their disappearance may have been inspired by religious intolerance against the group, simply because they were Christians.

The foursome formed the leadership team of St George's, the Anglican church in Baghdad, where Canon Andrew White, Director of the Foundation for Reconciliation in the Middle East, is vicar. The church had been closed for thirteen years until it reopened in 1993 after the Gulf War. Canon White told David Thomas of the *Daily Telegraph*: 'Tariq Aziz [the Iraqi deputy prime minister at the time, himself a Christian] let me take services there when I visited, but most of the congregation were spies. There'd be a few local Iraqis and some people from the UN, but in essence it was a Mukhabarat [Iraqi intelligence department] service.'[3]

A regular visitor to Baghdad since 1999, Canon White wrote enthusiastically about St George's in his review of 2004 for the International Centre for Reconciliation at Coventry Cathedral:

> The joy on the faces of the worshippers each Sunday was enough to spur my team and me on in our work of search for peace and hostages in growing chaos. Nothing though compared to the Palm Sunday Procession as the congregation encircled the church with cries of Hosanna; such vibrancy and life as they really pleaded with God to save them now. Despite many churches closing, St George's has remained open with a growing congregation and a wonderful lay pastor Maher running the church even when I am not there.[4]

Canon White developed a leadership team of Iraqis around him, led by Maher Dahkel with Firas as his deputy; Firas translated for Canon White when he preached. Maher's wife, Imaam Raheem, led the women's work and Yeheya led the worship.

When threats against Canon White made it impossible for him to reach the church, Maher took over running all the worship and the church grew to over 800.

In a letter to me written as this book goes to press in January 2006, Canon White writes:

> At the beginning of September 2005 the team of four went to a Church leaders' meeting in Amman, Jordan. On 12 September they headed back to Iraq. The last message we had from them was just prior to the entry to Rammadi at the beginning of the dangerous Al Anbar region. At first we hoped that they had been kidnapped. Many weeks have passed and still no

news. It looks increasingly likely that they were targeted because they were Christians. All intelligence points to this.

As the situation deteriorates in Iraq it is clear that Churches are being increasingly targeted as are all followers of Jesus. This is a very sad reality.

Ziwar Mohamad Ismaeel (?–2005), Zakho, Iraqi Kurdistan

Kurdish Christian Ziwar Mohamad Ismaeel was shot dead on 17 February 2005 in the city of Zakho in Iraqi Kurdistan.

Local sources reported that Ziwar, who was a taxi driver by profession, was killed with a machine gun by a man about 40 years old. Open Doors said that the motives of the killer were not known, although friends of the victim confirmed that after Ziwar's conversion several years ago, his openness about his Christian faith had caused controversy among local Muslims. He leaves behind a wife and five children.

From the beginning, Ziwar's relatives had strongly opposed his conversion. When Ziwar became a Christian, his family went to a local mullah to ask what to do, since he had left Islam. The mullah declared him an apostate and recommended he be killed. So some of his relatives captured him and took him out to a remote place, where they gave him the choice of either renouncing his faith or being killed.

However, some of Ziwar's friends managed to rescue him and spirit him away into hiding. But Ziwar refused to stay there very long as he did not want to show fear. 'With Jesus on my side, I have nothing to fear,' he commented at the time. 'I have to go back to my family to tell them that even when they kill me, I will never deny Christ.'

In the years that followed, Ziwar boldly testified to his new faith. Many of the passengers in his taxi heard the gospel, as he told everybody who wanted to listen.

In 2001, when he was arrested for the first time, policemen found three Bibles in his car. At the police station he was told that he would be killed if he did not return to Islam. However, he was released some two weeks later. When he returned home, his father was waiting there to shoot him on the spot.

Friends who witnessed the heated argument that broke out between family members thought Ziwar's last hour had come. Quickly, they collected his most precious belongings, including two boxes of Bibles and books, and fled with them to the church office. To their surprise, Ziwar showed up the following day to pick up his belongings. He was even a little displeased that his friends had doubted he would survive.

In May 2002, Ziwar was again arrested, allegedly for political reasons. During police interrogations he was told that some people did not like it that he was witnessing about Christ.

Towards the end he confided that he was being shadowed by some extremists, and the night before his death some Christians begged him to flee to safety. He refused, saying, 'No, my place is here. I will not hide.'

On the morning of 17 February 2005, a visitor came to the taxi centre and asked for Ziwar. Taxi drivers overheard him asking Ziwar to take tea with him nearby, and asking, 'Will you come back to Islam?' They distinctly recalled Ziwar saying, 'No, I am very happy in my faith.'

Moments later, after the two had left, shots rang out. The murderer opened fire on Ziwar at point-blank range. Eighteen bullets went into his face, ten into his chest. Ziwar died quickly. The murderer shouted, 'God is great' in Arabic and tried to flee, but other taxi drivers caught him. He is now in jail, and the local police chief is asking for the death penalty.

The murderer confessed in prison that he had a dream where the prophet Muhammad told him to kill Ziwar at the end of Ramadan, the Muslim month of fasting. He was assured that if he died in the attempt he would go to paradise. The murderer has two wives and ten children. Some fear that if he is released from jail, Ziwar's family will murder him.

Yet the believers of Zakho are not frightened as a result of Ziwar's martyrdom. Their pastor said, 'We have found that many people have come to us and said, "We are having to re-think our religion, because how can it be right to kill a good man like this? What kind of God is it that would be pleased by this?" And so we pray and hope that it will lead to a greater harvest for Christ in this town.'

He added quietly, 'That's what Ziwar would have wanted!'

Since the Gulf War of 1991, the church of Iraqi Kurdistan has experienced remarkable growth. Local authorities do not hinder church activities, but Islamic groups operating in the region have persistently threatened the Kurdish Christians.

Chapter 3

The fruit of persecution
in Israel

Polly Sigulim (escalating harassment, 2004–2005), Israel

Israel is the one country in the Middle East where the number of Christians has grown significantly in the last thirty years. Geoffrey Smith of Christian Friends of Israel (CFI) says, 'Most of the Christian population are Israeli Arabs, but the number of Jewish believers in Jesus has grown from 150 to about 10,000 since 1967. In the southern Israeli town of Arad they face harassment and persecution from the ultra-orthodox community.'

Messianic Jew Polly Sigulim is a widow, the mother of three children and five foster children. She rents a large home at the end of a street in Arad. Demonstrations have been held outside her home every week since April 2004 with demonstrators hurling religious and personal insults at Sigulim and her family.

On 12 September 2005 the Israeli High Court heard a petition by ultra-orthodox Jews to hold a 700-person demonstration in front of her house, Compass Direct reported. The ultra-orthodox group, the Gur Hassidim, was seeking to reverse a decision by the Israeli police to prohibit a demonstration in front of Sigulim's home.

Initially, when the weekly demonstrations began, Israeli police only watched as demonstrators hurled religious and personal insults at the family during demonstrations. Police had claimed that, because of the constitutional freedom of expression, they could not forbid smaller demonstrations in front of the houses of Sigulim, other Messianic Jewish believers and Christians. The subsequent ban came after dangerous escalations in harassment.

The weekly demonstrations started when an Israeli Jewish girl, who is a friend of the family, asked to be baptized. Some years ago the girl, who regularly visited the family, asked one of Sigulim's foster children for a New Testament. After reading it twice, she became a believer in Jesus.

'It was not a matter of Yakim [her pastor] or me preaching to her,' Sigulim recalls. 'She wanted what the other kids have.'

Because she was a minor, the congregation did not allow her to participate in its activities. When she turned 18, she wanted to be baptized. Four months later, in April 2004, 250 ultra-orthodox Jews held a big demonstration in front of Sigulim's house.

This demonstration left those present with 'very hard feelings and impressions,' said Yakim Figueras, pastor of the Hebrew-speaking congregation of Christians and Messianic Jews in Arad to which Sigulim belongs. 'There were hard words said against the believers. We were called worse than Israel's worst enemies through big loudspeakers.'

Since then, scores of small demonstrations have taken place near Sigulim's house, Figueras said.

'The demonstrations are intimidating,' he added. 'If they come to my house every day or every week to show people that here lives a dangerous missionary, then that is intimidating to my children. They do not do it quietly. They shout, scream, and give flyers with lies about us.'

Yakim was in court to hear the petition. He said Polly apologized for having a different belief and confessed her faith in the New Testament, as a Jewess. She told them about her children and foster children; two of her own boys were sitting in the front row in military uniform. She also explained that all the children under her foster care come from Messianic or Christian backgrounds.

Sigulim has said the ordeal has caused her and other families to become bolder and stronger in their faith: 'It has been a spiritual strengthening for everybody, including the youngest.'

Ahmad El-Achwal (murdered, January 2004), Askar Refugee Camp

Ahmad El-Achwal, one Palestinian convert to Christianity, was shot dead when he refused to revert to Islam. In a tribute to him, Justus Reid Weiner of the Jerusalem Center for Public Affairs wrote: 'El-Achwal was a married father of eight who lived in the Askar Refugee Camp. Despite repeated harsh treatment at the hands of the Palestinian Authority including imprisonment, severe beatings, arson, intimidation and torture, El-Achwal clung to his religious [Christian] beliefs and even ran an informal church in his house. El-Achwal was murdered on 21 January 2004, at the entrance to his residence.' His death highlighted the religious tension between Muslims and Christians in the region.

In Gaza, Pastor Hanna Massad of Gaza Baptist Church has expressed concern over the safety of Palestinian Christians: 'We are worried that during this transition period different groups may fight one another,' he said, 'and whether the Palestinian forces are strong enough to deal with it.'

The Christian village of Taibe in the West Bank was attacked in September 2005 by 'a crowd of 500 Muslim men chanting Allu Akhbar', a resident reported. 'They poured kerosene on many buildings and set them on fire. Many of the attackers broke into houses and stole furniture, jewellery and electrical appliances.'

'It was like a war,' said another resident. 'They arrived in groups and many of them were holding clubs'.

Reporting on the situation, Geoffrey Smith from Christian Friends of Israel (CFI) said,

> So long as Israel remained in occupation of Gaza, criticism of conditions under the Palestinian Authority (PA) could be deflected into criticism of Israel. Withdrawal of Israeli forces changes the situation and leaves different Palestinian factions contending for power. It also enables Christian leaders in Gaza and the West Bank to speak more openly about their concerns

and fears without being afraid of accusations that they are acting as stooges for Israel if they speak openly of persecution.

A dossier relating incidents of violence and intimidation by Muslim extremists has been handed over to church authorities in Jerusalem. According to a report from Bethlehem it includes 93 alleged incidents of abuse by an 'Islamic fundamentalist mafia' – gangs of thugs who shelter under the name of Islam. It also details 140 cases of land theft in which Christians were forced off their land by gangs backed by corrupt officials under the Palestinian Authority.

The numerical decline of the Christian community in the district of Bethlehem, from a majority to just 10 per cent, has often been blamed on Israel's security measures by her critics. 'These reports show another side to the story, which has long been known, but kept quiet for fear that criticism could rebound to further the disadvantage of the Christian minority,' Smith says.

He adds, 'In practice, Christian families are typically smaller and better educated than their Muslim counterparts in Bethlehem and are therefore more mobile internationally. It is hard for them to remain under the Palestinian Authority in face of continued persecution, land theft, threats and abuse from lawless gangs, so many have fled to North America rather than remain to struggle.'

The draft constitution for a State of Palestine decrees that Islam shall be the official religion and the principles of sharia shall be a major source of legislation. Sharia forbids a Muslim to change his religion on pain of either recantation or death.[1] While the state will guarantee free access to shrines, there is no guarantee of freedom to change religion. The draft constitution states that Christianity and all other monotheistic religions shall be equally revered and respected, but when a moderate Muslim imam in Bethlehem called for an end to the anti-Christian discrimination and land grabs, he was repeatedly threatened by militant extremists, Smith reports.

Salim Munayer (b. 1955), Bethlehem

Salim Munayer reflects the complexity of nationality, religion, language and culture in the region.

He and his family live in Jerusalem, but as a Palestinian Arab Christian citizen of Israel, he says, 'I am a minority twice over, once as an Arab among Israeli Jews, and second as an Arab Christian among Arab Muslims.'

Salim was born in Israel into a Greek Orthodox Palestinian family. He attended several different primary schools (Catholic, Jewish and Arabic), and was attending a Jewish high school when the 1973 war broke out. 'It was through a Bible study attended by a mixed group of Jewish and Arab students that I became a [Christian] believer,' he says. 'At that time [1977, when he was 22], there weren't any messianic congregations really, so I became part of the moving of the Holy Spirit among young Israelis. Many young Jews were coming to Christ, so I found myself, an Arab, helping plant messianic congregations!'

After graduating from Tel Aviv University, Salim went to the USA to study New Testament and Missiology and returned to Israel in 1985 to teach at Bethlehem Bible College, where he is now the academic dean. The focus of his Ph.D. in 2000 was the ethnic identity of Palestinian Arab Christians in Israel.

Having lived in Israel among the Jewish community for much of his life, going to Bethlehem to work was a revelation, Salim says. 'For the first time I was really exposed to the situation of the Palestinian Christians in general. I saw all the injustices and realized that the media was not reflecting reality on this.'

Crossing from work in Bethlehem to his home and family in Jerusalem has, at times, been life-threatening – especially during the violent conflicts of the Intifada (Arabic for uprising).

As well as working at the Bible college, Salim was also involved in a Hebrew training programme taking Messianic believers from discipleship to leadership. 'Because I was teaching Palestinian believers in Bethlehem and Jewish believers in Tel Aviv, I suddenly saw the gap in understanding. Both groups were believers but they were living in two different worlds.

Most of them had never met a believer from the "other" camp,' says Salim.

'The whole concept of Jewish believers was so new it was really a surprise,' he explains. 'The Palestinian Christians thought, "Oh, they're Christians, they'll understand." But we didn't realize how complex their relationship was with the historical church, even with the word "Christian". It got to the point where believers didn't want to meet together because of all the political and theological arguments.'

Observing this impasse prompted Salim to develop an organization named Musalaha – an Arabic word which means forgiveness and reconciliation. Musalaha grew out of Salim's longing to demonstrate the reconciliation all believers have in Christ.

'I came to the conclusion that Jewish and Palestinian believers needed to be brought together face to face,' he says. 'Anything less would not work because of the dehumanization and demonization going on from both sides.' Desert Encounters – life-changing events where Palestinians and Israelis share the challenge of a desert journey – have formed the melting pot for Musalaha's reconciliation efforts.

Salim describes the desert as, 'not Jewish . . . not Palestinian . . . not a classroom or a church. We're stuck there. We can't run away. It's like putting a man in a microwave. We've seen people with really extreme political opinions. After one day in the desert, there's a real change, a visible openness. It's amazing. You throw them into the desert and something happens. Functioning together in the hardship of the desert, climbing, hiking, sharing water and food, and dealing with the basic needs of everyday life, highlights the reality that we are all created in [God's] image. Travelling together in the harsh desert, we need to encourage each other through acts of faith. These acts are only possible because we are a new creation in Christ, created henceforth in His image.'

These desert encounters bring together people of very different backgrounds. On one trip to the desert in Jordan, twenty-seven people from Galilee, Haifa, Jerusalem and the West Bank took part. Geographically the area they came from is not much bigger than the south-east corner of England, but within the group were people whose mother tongue was Arabic, Hebrew, Russian or English; no language was common to all. Passports spoke of the group's complexity: Israeli – both Jewish and Arabic, Palestinian (for those from the West Bank) and Jordanian (for Palestinians living in East Jerusalem). And when the two from East Jerusalem reached the Jordanian border, they were turned away, in spite of their Jordanian passports. The reason given was that ten days before, the Israeli Minister of the Interior had made a decision to refuse work and entry visas for Jordanians to work in the construction industry in Eilat in Israel. They were victims of a political 'tit-for-tat'.

Chapter 4

Iran's saints and martyrs – a faithful remnant

Three Iranian Christian leaders died in suspicious circumstances in 1994.

Bishop Haik Hovsepian-Mehr, one of those who died, was
an outspoken advocate of religious liberty in his country. He
did not believe in succumbing to government pressure and
chose instead to tell the world about the plight of Iranian Christians. His fellow Assemblies of God minister, Hussein Soodmand, had been executed in December 1990 after a sharia court
condemned him for apostasy. According to Elam Ministries,
Bishop Haik said: 'If we go to jail or die for our faith, we want
the whole Christian world to know what is happening to their
brothers and sisters.'

A memorial service to pay tribute to the life of Bishop Haik
Hovsepian-Mehr was held in London on 17 February 1994. In
tribute to Bishop Haik, David Alton MP – now Lord Alton –
issued this challenge: 'Jesus said that greater love has no man
than to lay down one's life for a friend and Bishop Haik gave
real expression to this by placing his own life at risk when he
stepped in on behalf of his friend Mehdi Dibaj. He took the risk
and paid the ultimate price. We in the West must now make
certain that his sacrifice leads to a massive campaign for freedom
of worship in Iran – the finest memorial he can have.'

Haik Hovsepian-Mehr (1945–1994), Iran

Bishop Haik actively campaigned for the release of Revd Mehdi
Dibaj, who had been condemned to death on 21 December
1993. Dibaj had been a Christian for 45 years, and had been in
prison for nine years, Elam Ministries reported. However, on
Wednesday 19 January 1994, just three days after the govern-

ment released Mehdi Dibaj from prison, Bishop Haik disappeared.

According to government officials in Iran, Bishop Haik's body was found by the police in one of the suburbs of Tehran on 20 January. He had been stabbed several times in the chest. After keeping the body for several days, they went ahead and buried him in the large Muslim cemetery just outside Tehran, as they had not been able to identify him.

The family were eventually notified on 30 January and the authorities gave permission for the body to be returned to the family. A Christian burial took place in the presence of over 2,000 people in Tehran on 3 February. However, in the words of one observer, 'Haik's love for Muslims was so great that he was allowed to lie in a Muslim cemetery for three days.' At the end of the Christian ceremony a Catholic priest, with tears in his eyes, took a shovel and started throwing earth onto the coffin, saying, 'This man is a saint and a martyr.'

Bishop Haik Hovsepian–Mehr was born into an Armenian family in Tehran on 6 January 1945. From childhood, he experienced many difficulties, including poverty, a sick mother and the separation of his parents, but at the age of 14, through the help of older believers, he became a Christian. From the outset he wanted to serve Christ, and as soon as he completed school in 1962, he began helping to pastor a church in Majidieh, a suburb in East Tehran.

A year later, he entered military service and was sent to northern Iran. During this time he established a church in his home in the town of Gonbade Kavoos and spent the evenings teaching his Christian faith. As a result, some were converted and baptized. Following the completion of military service, he was invited into full-time ministry and began his work as pastor of the Majidieh and Narmak churches in East Tehran. It was during this time that the Majidieh church building was extended to twice its previous size.

While at Majidieh, he went to Isfahan for a time, where he met his future wife, Takoosh; they were married in 1967. He was ordained, at the age of 22, by a group of pastors to serve at the Majidieh church. The following year, 1968, Haik and his wife moved to the city of Gorgan in northern Iran and worked for fourteen years in an area which was spiritually very difficult.

They faced a personal tragedy in 1969 when their six-month-old son was killed in a car accident along with the three children of a missionary family. In fact both Haik and his wife were seriously injured but they both made a remarkable recovery. As they continued their ministry in Gorgan, a church was started there.

In 1980, they moved to Tehran, where Haik served as assistant to the superintendent of the Assemblies of God, Revd Leon Hairapetian. In 1982 Haik was appointed superintendent of the Assemblies of God Churches in Iran; it was in this capacity that he was known in Iran as a bishop.

During his twelve years as superintendent, Bishop Haik travelled widely throughout the country encouraging the church leaders. He was also involved in a wide range of activities, including representing the churches before the Islamic authorities; coordinating relief and development, especially following the influx of refugees into Iran from Iraq and the earthquake in northern Iran; giving direction to the many church committees and the local Bible school in Tehran. During his time as superintendent, seven people were ordained to the ministry, seven appointed as elders and many more as deacons. Also, with his support and encouragement a large number of Christian believers entered various church ministries throughout the country as well as some outside of Iran. Bishop Haik was also a musician and singer, writing many Christian songs in Farsi and Armenian as well as making a number of recordings.

Bishop Haik's influence extended well beyond his own denomination. One of his main contributions was to bring into closer cooperation all the Protestant churches in Iran and when the Council of the Pastors of the Iranian Protestant Churches was established in 1987, he was appointed its chairman – a position he held until his death. This enabled him to have a wider role in representing all the Protestant churches before the government authorities as well as working with all the church leaders.

In more recent times the Church in Iran has experienced increased harassment and pressure from the authorities, which have imposed many restrictions on Church activities, persecution of Muslim converts and the closure of some churches. Therefore Bishop Haik increasingly found himself having to relate to the government authorities over the violation of religious freedom in Iran. It was in this role that he campaigned for the release of Revd Dibaj.

After his death, Elam Ministries reported Church leaders in Iran as saying:

> Certainly this martyrdom and this sacrificial and mysterious death took place because of his beliefs, spiritual perception and his way of life. On the one hand our hearts are broken and torn because we have temporarily lost such a great personality with such a high spiritual calling who in every respect brought honour to the Church in Iran from around the world. But on the other hand, his courage inspires all God's servants and the Church in Iran to a greater zeal and bravery so that we will follow the way of Christ more faithfully, carrying the cross and denying ourselves.
>
> We will never forget his guidance, sermons, teaching and pleasant songs. May his spirit rest in joy, his memory remain dear and his love be in our hearts for ever.

The following verse was printed on the programme cover of the memorial service held in Tehran on 7 February 1994: 'Unless a grain of wheat falls to the ground and dies, it remains only a single seed. But if it dies, it produces many seeds' (John 12:24). The blood of the martyrs is the seed of the Church.

Tateos Michaelian (?–1994), Iran

After Bishop Haik's death, Tateos Michaelian, the senior pastor of St John's Armenian Evangelical (Presbyterian) Church, succeeded him as chairman of the Council of Protestant Ministers.

Michaelian was last seen alive leaving his home in Tehran during the afternoon of 29 June 1994 in response to a telephone call, Jubilee Campaign reports. The call allegedly came from his self-confessed assassin Farahnaz Anami, a woman who had, on earlier occasions, attended his church professing an interest in Christianity. According to official reports, his body was found inside a freezer in a private house in Majidieh rented by Anami and she, allegedly, implicated at least one other female accomplice to the murder. The cause of death was multiple gunshot wounds to the head. Members of his family positively identified the body at the public mortuary on 2 July.

Middle East Concern (MEC) reports that its sources have revealed that Tateos' body had in fact been dismembered and that a copy of a 'hit list' of prominent Christians was found with his remains. MEC's sources, who have access to high-level government contacts, categorically state that they believe that the murders of all three Christian leaders were carried out by a death squad operating within the Iranian security structures and sanctioned by orders from the highest political levels. They further believe that Anami (if she was the killer) is, in fact, a government agent and not a member of the MKO (Mujahedin Khalq Organization, an armed group attempting to overthrow the Iranian regime) as the authorities allege.

Mehdi Dibaj (1934–1994), Iran

'I would rather have the whole world against me, but know the Almighty God is with me; be called an apostate, but know I have the approval of the God of glory.'

These are the words of Mehdi Dibaj to the court which pronounced his death sentence. After spending nine years in an Iranian prison on the charge of apostasy, he was tried in December 1993, found guilty and sentenced to death.

The court verdict reads: 'at the age of 19 he has chosen the religion of Christianity . . . because of his non-repentance and his insistence on his non-Islamic belief . . . he is sentenced to execution.'

Due to pressure from human rights groups Mehdi Dibaj was released in January 1994, but he was found murdered on 5 July 1994. This is his last testament, given before the Islamic court in December 1993, made available to us by Elam Ministries.

In the holy name of God who is our life and existence.

With all humility I express my gratitude to the Judge of all heaven and earth for this precious opportunity, and with brokenness I wait upon the Lord to deliver me from this court trial according to His promises. I also beg the honoured members of the court present to listen with patience to my defence and with respect for the Name of the Lord.

I am a Christian, a sinner who believes Jesus has died for my sins on the cross and who by His resurrection and victory over death, has made me righteous in the presence of the Holy God. The true God speaks about this fact in His Holy Word, the Gospel. Jesus means Saviour, 'because He will save His people from their sins'. Jesus paid the penalty of our sins by His own blood and gave us a new life so that we can live for the glory of God by the help of the Holy Spirit and be like a dam against corruption, be a channel of blessing and healing, and be protected by the love of God.

In response to this kindness, He has asked me to deny myself and be His fully surrendered follower, and not fear people, even if they kill my body. I have been charged with 'Apostasy'. The invisible God who knows our hearts has given assurance to us Christians that we are not among the apostates who will perish, but among the believers so we may save our lives. In Islamic law an apostate is one who does not believe in God, the prophets or the resurrection of the dead. We Christians believe in all three!

They say, 'You were a Muslim and you have become a Christian.' No, for many years I had no religion. After searching and studying I accepted God's call and I believed in the Lord Jesus Christ in order to receive eternal life. People choose their religion, but a Christian is chosen by Christ. He says, 'You have not chosen me but I have chosen you.' From when? Before the foundation of the world.

People say, 'You were a Muslim from your birth.' God says, 'You were a Christian from the beginning.' He states that He chose us thousands of years ago, even before the creation of the universe, so that through the sacrifice of Jesus Christ we may be His! A Christian means one who belongs to Jesus Christ.

The eternal God, who sees the end from the beginning and who has chosen me to belong to Him, knew from everlasting whose heart would be drawn to Him and who would be willing to sell their faith and eternity for a pot of porridge.

I would rather have the whole world against me, but know the Almighty God is with me; be called an apostate, but know I have the approval of the God of glory.

The Almighty God will raise up anyone He chooses and bring down others; accept some and reject others; send some to heaven and others to hell. Now because God does whatever He desires, who can separate us from the love of God? Or who can destroy the relationship between the Creator and the creature?

Our refuge is the mercy seat of God who is exalted from the beginning. I know in whom I have believed, and He is able to guard what I have entrusted to Him to the end, until I reach the Kingdom of God, the place where the righteous shine like the sun, but where the evildoers will receive their punishment in hellfire.

They tell me, 'Return!' But from the arms of my God, who can I return to? Is it right to accept what people are saying instead of obeying the Word of God? It is now 45 years that I am walking with the God of miracles, and His kindness upon me is like a shadow and I owe Him much for His fatherly love and concern.

The love of Jesus has filled all my being and I feel the warmth of His love in every part of my body. God, who is my glory and honour and protector, has put His seal of approval upon me through His unsparing blessings and miracles.

The good and kind God reproves and punishes all those whom He loves. He tests them in preparation for heaven. The God of Daniel, who protected His friends in the fiery furnace, has protected me for nine years in prison and all the bad happenings have turned out for our good and gain, so much so that I am filled to overflowing with joy and thankfulness.

The God of Job has tested my faith and commitment in order to strengthen my patience and faithfulness. During those nine years He has freed me from all my responsibilities so that under the protection of His blessed Name I would spend my time in prayer and study of His Word, with heart-searching and brokenness, and grow in the knowledge of my Lord. I praise the Lord for this unique opportunity. 'You gave me space in my confinement, my difficult hardships brought healing and your kindnesses revived me'. Oh what great blessings God has in store for those who fear Him!

They object to my evangelising. But, 'If you find a blind person near a well and keep silent then you have sinned' [a Persian proverb]. It is our religious duty, as long as the door of God's mercy is open, to convince evildoers to turn from their sinful ways and find refuge in Him in order to be saved from the wrath of a Righteous God and from the coming dreadful punishment.

Jesus Christ says, 'I am the door. Whoever enters through me will be saved.' 'I am the way, the truth and the life. No one comes to the Father except through Me.' 'Salvation is found in no one else, for there is no other name under heaven given to men by which we must be saved.' Among the prophets of God, only Jesus Christ rose from the dead and He is our living intercessor for ever.

He is our Saviour and He is the Son of God. To know Him means to know eternal life. I, a useless sinner, have believed in His beloved person and all His words and miracles recorded in the Gospel, and I have committed my life into His hands. Life for me is an opportunity to serve Him, and death is a better opportunity to be with Christ. Therefore I am not only satisfied to be in prison for the honour of His Holy Name, but am ready to give my life for the sake of Jesus my Lord and enter His kingdom sooner, the place where the elect of God enter everlasting life, but the wicked to eternal damnation.

May the shadow of God's kindness and His hand of blessing and healing be upon you and remain for ever. Amen.

With respect,

Your Christian prisoner

Mehdi Dibaj[1]

Europe VII

Chapter 1

Obedient to God under Nazi persecution

Christians in Europe have also suffered persecution and death because of their Christian faith. Obedience to God has been more important for them than obedience to any other authority.

Dietrich Bonhoeffer, Maximilian Kolbe and members of the ten Boom family are examples of Christians who were martyred under the Nazi regime.

Dietrich Bonhoeffer (1906–1945), Germany

Dietrich Bonhoeffer was hanged in the concentration camp at Flossenbürg on 9 April 1945, because of his participation in the Protestant resistance movement and failed plots to assassinate Hitler. Although the charge against him was political, his resistance grew directly from his understanding both of the Bible and the nature of the Church; he died because he acted on those Christian beliefs.

In her profile of Bonhoeffer, journalist Mary Craig highlights the central question posed in his book *The Cost of Discipleship: 'What does it mean to be a disciple of Christ in today's world?'* His response: 'discipleship demands a total response. Lip service or mere membership of a Church could not be enough'. Quoting from the book, Craig adds, 'The victory over hatred which the cross represents is the life-long task of the Christian, and to achieve it, it is not enough to pay lip service to Christ or to declare oneself a member of the Church . . . Such love as this can only be the fruit of grace, that grace which must be sought for and which costs us everything . . . Such grace ... is costly because it costs a man his life; and it is grace because it gives a man the only true life.'[1]

Bonhoeffer was born in Breslau, Germany (now Wroclaw, Poland). He received a doctorate in theology in Berlin and was ordained as a Lutheran pastor. As Hitler came to power, Bonhoeffer was an outspoken opponent of the Nazi influence on the Church in Germany. While some German Christians looked on Hitler as a saviour, Bonhoeffer and other reformers like Martin Niemoller formed the Pastors' Emergency League, pledging themselves to be true to the Bible.

Bonhoeffer accused the Church of being silent when it should have cried out. In 1939 he was offered a job in New York. He could have escaped war-torn Europe, but declined the offer, preferring to share the difficulties faced by his fellow Germans rather than enjoying the peace and security of an overseas academic appointment.

He was arrested on conspiracy charges in April 1943 after money used to help Jews escape to Switzerland was traced to him. He spent 18 months in a military prison in Berlin where he enjoyed a measure of freedom, receiving letters and parcels from family. Although his letters sometimes spoke of his inner turmoil, he is said to have appeared calm and cheerful, comforting and helping fellow prisoners.

In April 1944 he wrote to his friend Eberhard Bethge, 'I'm convinced . . . that my life has followed a straight and unbroken course, at any rate in its outward conduct. It has been an uninterrupted enrichment of experience for which I can only be thankful. If my life were to end here and now, in these conditions, that would have a meaning that I think I could understand; on the other hand, everything might be a thorough preparation for a new start and a new task when peace comes.'[2]

Prison gave him time to develop his understanding of what it was to be a Christian. He wrote confidently to Bethge: 'all things are possible with God . . . no earthly power can touch us without His will . . . danger and distress can only drive us closer to Him.'[3]

In his last letter, on 23 August 1944, he wrote:

You must never doubt that I'm travelling with gratitude and cheerfulness along the road where I'm being led. My past life is brimfull of God's goodness, and my sins are covered by the forgiving love of Christ crucified. I'm most thankful for the people I've met, and I only hope that they never have to grieve about me, but that they too will always be certain of, and thankful for, God's mercy and forgiveness. Forgive my writing this. Don't let it grieve or upset you for a moment, but let it make you happy.[4]

In October 1944, when his connection to the 20 July assassination attempt on Hitler became known, he was moved to the notorious Prinz Albrechtstrasse Gestapo prison in Berlin. From there, in February 1945, he was taken to Buchenwald, where a fellow prisoner, Captain Payne Best, a British officer, said, 'his soul really shone in the dark desperation of our prison . . . [he was] all humility and sweetness – he always seemed to diffuse an atmosphere of happiness, of joy in every smallest event in life, and of deep gratitude for the mere fact that he was alive . . . He was one of the very few men I have ever seen to whom his God was real and close to him.'[5]

When the SS arrived to take him away he whispered a message for his English friend Bishop George Bell: 'Tell him that for me this is the end, but also the beginning.'[6]

He was moved to the Flossenbürg concentration camp, where an all-night trial sentenced him to death. He was hanged the next day, only two weeks before the camp was liberated.

The SS doctor who witnessed Bonhoeffer's death watched him kneeling in prayer and said, 'I was most deeply moved by the way this loveable man was praying, so devoutly and so sure that God heard him. At the place of execution he again said a short prayer and then climbed the steps to the gallows, brave and composed. His death ensued after a few seconds. In the almost fifty years I worked as a doctor, I hardly ever saw a man die so submissive to the will of God.'

Martin Niemoller (1892–1984), Germany

One of Bonhoeffer's friends, Martin Niemoller, also suffered for his faith under the Nazi regime, but survived. He wrote a poem, which exists in a variety of versions, warning about the consequences of not opposing tyranny – a warning which Bonhoeffer and others like him took to heart.

> First they came for the communists, and I did not speak
>   out –
> because I was not a communist;
> Then they came for the socialists, and I did not speak out –
> because I was not a socialist;
> Then they came for the trade unionists, and I did not
>   speak out –
> because I was not a trade unionist;
> Then they came for the Jews, and I did not speak out –
> because I was not a Jew;
> Then they came for me –
> and there was no one left to speak up for me.

Maximilian Kolbe (1894–1941), Poland

Maximilian Kolbe was a Polish priest who died as prisoner 16770 in Auschwitz, on 14 August 1941.

He was arrested in February 1941 by the Gestapo for sheltering refugees – including 2,000 Jews – in the monastery he had founded near Warsaw. On 25 May he was transferred from the local prison to Auschwitz concentration camp. When a fellow-prisoner escaped from the bunker they shared, the Nazis selected ten others to be killed by starvation in reprisal for the alleged escape (the 'escapee' was found later, drowned in a latrine).

One of the ten selected to die, Franciszek Gajowniczek, began to cry: 'My wife! My children! I will never see them again!'

At this, Maximilian Kolbe stepped forward and asked to die in his place. His request was granted. Kolbe and three of the others survived two weeks' starvation – they were then executed by lethal injection.

Kolbe was canonized by Pope John Paul II on 10 October 1982, in the presence of Franciszek Gajowniczek, the man whose place he took and who was still alive.

The ten Boom family (arrested, 28 February 1944), Netherlands

'There is no pit so deep that God's love is not deeper still.' When Betsie ten Boom spoke these words to her sister Corrie, both women were prisoners in the infamous Ravensbruck concentration camp located near Berlin, Germany. Betsie died there. She was 59.

'God will give us the love to be able to forgive our enemies,' Betsie told her sister before she died. Corrie admitted later that she found those words difficult to believe.

The ten Boom family lived in Haarlem during the Second World War. Putting their Christian faith into practice, they made their home a refuge for people in need: Jews, members of the Dutch underground resistance movement and other fugitives from the Nazis. An estimated 800 lives were saved by the family. But, on 28 February 1944, they were betrayed.

In a Gestapo raid, Betsie and Corrie were arrested together with their father Casper, Corrie's brother Willem, sister Nollie and nephew Peter. Four Jews and two underground workers remained undetected in a hiding place behind a false wall. The four Jews were taken later to new 'safe houses', and three survived the war. One of the underground workers was killed during the war years, but the other survived.

Casper ten Boom, who was 84, died ten days later in Scheveningen Prison. When asked if he knew he could die for helping Jews, he is said to have replied, 'It would be an honor to give my life for God's ancient people.'[7]

Sixty-year-old Willem was also jailed. In prison, he contracted spinal tuberculosis and died shortly after the war.

Corrie and Betsie spent ten months in three different prisons; Ravensbruck was the last. Betsie grew steadily weaker and died on 16 December 1944. Some of her last words to Corrie were, '[we] must tell them what we have learned here. We must tell them that there is no pit so deep that He is not deeper still. They will listen to us, Corrie, because we have been here.'[8]

Due to a clerical error, Corrie was released from Ravensbruck one week before all women her age were killed. She left Germany vowing never to return, but later was invited back on a speaking engagement. Her first talk was on forgiveness. Suddenly, as she was speaking, she saw one of her former prison guards sitting in the audience. At the end of her talk he approached her with a beaming smile. 'How grateful I am for your message, *Fraulein*,' he said. 'To think that, as you say, He has washed my sins away!'

Taking his hand, when he stretched it out towards hers, says Corrie, was the hardest thing she had ever had to do in her life. But, she says,

> As I took his hand the most incredible thing happened. From my shoulder along my arm and through my hand a current seemed to pass from me to him, while into my heart sprang a love for this stranger that almost overwhelmed me.
>
> And so I discovered . . . when He tells us to love our enemies, He gives, along with the command, the love itself.[9]

Chapter 2
Eastern Europe's giants against injustice

Under communism, atheists sought to stamp out all traces of Christian faith and practice from Eastern Europe. Churches were closed. Priests and church leaders were persecuted, imprisoned and killed. Christians lived in fear of betrayal to the ever-watchful secret police. Romania, Czechoslovakia and Albania are only three examples of countries where Christians were forced to keep their faith secret, or face severe consequences.

Alexandru Todea (1912–2002), Romania

'You have no power to fight me. I risk nothing, because I have nothing to lose – not work, not money, not even my freedom.'

This is what the Romanian cleric Cardinal Alexandru Todea said to a Romanian secret policeman who was pressurizing him to renounce his Christian faith. Michael Bourdeaux, of the Keston Institute, recorded the incident in Todea's obituary in the *Guardian* on 2 July 2002. Bourdeaux wrote:

> Cardinal Alexandru Todea, who has died just short of his 90th birthday, addressed these words to the Romanian secret police in 1979, when they tried yet again to force him to recant.
>
> Twenty-eight years earlier, on 31 January 1951, they had burst into the flat where the then bishop, recently consecrated in secret, had been hiding for two years, following escape after his first arrest. He heard them coming, and bolted into a hole under the floorboards. They could not find him, but knew he had been there, so they occupied themselves playing cards above his motionless body, thinking they were awaiting his return.

Deep into the night, a specialist search unit found Todea, stuck head first in his hideout. Thus began four decades of imprisonment, house arrest or confinement to his town of Raghin, in Transylvania.

After the execution of the Romanian dictator Nicolae Ceausescu on Christmas Day 1989, Todea, by then 77, began a new life. Over the next two years, before a stroke paralysed him, he worked ceaselessly for the restoration of the legality of his Byzantine-Rite Catholic church and the restitution of its property, which the communists had confiscated and trans-ferred to the Orthodox church 40 years earlier.

Todea was born near Targu Mures, then in the Austro-Hungarian empire. His father was a shepherd, who tried to persuade him that his life would be on the land. He made his own way to Blaj, where the Assumptionist Fathers befriended him and sponsored his theological studies, which were so successful that he was sent for seven years to Rome, where he rubbed shoulders with students from all over the world.

Ordination to the priesthood of the Byzantine-Rite Catholic church followed his return in 1939, though it would be more than 50 years before Rome could proclaim him Cardinal Archbishop of the region.

Metropolitan Alexandru Nicolescu of Blaj recognised Fr Todea's calibre and invited him to become his secretary. From 1940, he was professor of theology at Blaj, and, from 1945, chairman of the Raghin deanery. He became a bishop in 1950.

Once imprisoned by the communist regime, which was entrenched in power after Romania became a Soviet satellite in 1948, Todea emerged as one of the most outstanding of a generation of clergy in the Soviet bloc whose rock-like endurance ensured the survival of their faith. Humiliation – as head of the latrine brigade (though he continued to hear con-fessions, broom in hand); torture – standing in chains in the baking sun for seven days almost without food and water; isolation – during his decades of house arrest: none of these could break his spirit.

Immediately after Ceausescu's death, he set up contacts

with the new regime, and was received by Professor Dumitru Mazilu, vice-president of the National Salvation Front, to whom he broached the problem of the restitution of church rights. The meeting went well, but frustrations were to follow, and Todea never did win his case; the Orthodox church wanted each parish to hold a local referendum, which was unacceptable to him. He insisted that the government had confiscated them, so the government must give them back.

However, Todea was a peacemaker, and constantly urged Orthodox and Catholics to concentrate on the common spiritual values which united them. His approach found sympathetic ears in the person of Pope John Paul II, and was a key factor enabling the Pope, in 1999, to make his historic first visit to a predominantly Orthodox country.

Todea could not be at the airport to greet the pontiff [he had been paralysed by a stroke], but the first words the Pope spoke on Romanian soil were a tribute directly to him: 'The communist regime suppressed the church of the Byzantine Romanian Rite united with Rome, and persecuted bishops and priests, men and women, religious and lay people, many of whom paid with blood for their fidelity to Christ. Some survived the torture, and are still with us.

'My heartfelt thoughts turn to the worthy and beloved Cardinal Alexandru Todea, who spent 16 years in prison and 27 under house arrest.'

The Pope went on to honour the confessors and martyrs of the Orthodox and other churches. But the clarity of his statement would have been unthinkable without the groundwork laid by Cardinal Todea. He was one of the twentieth century's spiritual giants.

Stepan Trochta (1905–1974), Czechoslovakia

Cardinal Stepan Trochta died in Czechoslovakia the day after undergoing a brutal interrogation by the local official for religious affairs. Catholics in Czechoslovakia saw his death as martyrdom.

He trained in Italy and joined the Salesian order. After ordination in 1932 he was sent to Monrovia where he worked as a teacher, particularly with Czechoslovakian young people of all denominations. He was arrested by the Gestapo in 1942 and spent the war years in German prisons and concentration camps.

Michael Bourdeaux, who wrote a report on the life and death of the cardinal for the Keston Institute, dated 20 July 1974, said:

> His most harrowing experience was in Mauthausen, where he was tortured and shot and finally thrown onto a carriage full of dead bodies. Miraculously, he fell off the truck, recovered consciousness and found enough strength to return to his place of detention. In 1944 he came to Dachau where his knowledge of languages led to his becoming a kind of liaison officer between the various national groups of prisoners, their spiritual mainstay and even their physical welfare officer.

After the liberation of Czechoslovakia by the US forces, Dr Trochta was made Bishop of Litomerice by the pope in 1947. His motto was 'Labour, sacrifice, love'.

When the communists seized power in 1948, Bishop Trochta kept out of politics but continued preaching. In 1951 he was arrested and interrogated by the police for three years. Bourdeaux said, 'Afterwards he called this the most horrible period of his life.'

In 1954 he was sentenced to 25 years' forced labour for alleged high treason and espionage for the Vatican. His health gave way under the strain of hard labour. First he succumbed to tuberculosis; then he suffered a heart attack. Towards the end of 1960, he was temporarily released, but was forced to live as a layman. No one dared to give him permanent work so he lived on the lowest wage. When he went to communion wearing his worn-out working clothes, a few Christians recognized him. Food and clothes were sent to his lodgings but, as a result, he was re-arrested and imprisoned for a further six years. He then remained under house arrest until the Prague Spring of 1968, when Alexander Dubček became party leader, introducing his reforms as 'Socialism with a human face'.

Trochta was then allowed to resume his office, though with many restrictions. When the Archbishop of Prague, Cardinal Beran, died in 1969, Bishop Trochta was secretly made a cardinal by the pope. The appointment was made official in 1973, but Trochta continued to suffer ill-health and an unsuccessful eye operation in 1974 left him half blind.

Michael Bourdeaux continues the story:

> On 5 April 1974 [Trochta] received a visit from Dlabal, the local official for religious affairs. Dlabal had for some time been following all the Cardinal's activities. On a number of previous occasions he had talks with him and had behaved in a most arrogant manner. He was fully informed about the Cardinal's state of health and that the doctor had ordered complete rest and warned against any excitement. Dlabal had orders to force the Cardinal to remove the Salesians from the diocese and to transfer or suspend a number of zealous priests. The Cardinal refused. Dlabal threatened him in the most brutal fashion: 'Old fool, I'll break your bones if you don't send away the Salesian gang.' The 'conversation' lasted from 11.30 a.m. until 5.30 p.m. The Cardinal went to bed totally exhausted and spent a most uncomfortable night. In the morning he suffered a stroke and died that same afternoon.
>
> Roman Catholics in Czechoslovakia regard Cardinal Trochta as a martyr. For that reason the authorities made every effort to prevent public demonstrations on 17 April, the day of his funeral.

Albania's persecuted church (1944–1985)

Enver Hoxha came to power in Albania in November 1944 and remained president until his death in 1985. He declared himself an orthodox Marxist-Leninist and strongly admired Joseph Stalin. In 1960, Hoxha aligned Albania with the People's Republic of China in the Sino–Soviet split, severing relations with Moscow the following year. Then, in 1967, he proclaimed that Albania was the first atheist state in history. According to a report of the Free Albanian Committee in New York, by 1968 some 200 clergymen had been executed or sent to labour camps.

In 1985 the *Albanian Catholic Bulletin* published details of persecution under the rule of Enver Hoxha.[1] Here are the names and some brief information about a few of those who died. These stark facts offer a glimpse of the horrific suffering faced by Christians living in this brutal era of Albania's history.

December 1944: Franciscan Father Leke (Alexander) Luli is murdered by Yugoslav–Albanian Communist guerilla forces. According to a British war commander, his captors cut Luli's throat and dumped him in an unmarked grave in Kosova.

March 1945: Distinguished poet and humanist Father Lazer Shantoja is mercilessly tortured and shot.

December 1945: Father Ndre (Andrew) Zadeja, a poet and writer, is tortured and shot without trial.

February 1946: Franciscan Father Anton Harapi is executed after a mock trial.

March 1946: Jesuit Vice Provincial, Gjon Fausti, Rector of the Pontifical Seminary, Daniel Dajani, Franciscan Father Gjon Shllaku, and seminarian Mark Cuni, are executed after mock trial.

January 1947: Sigurimi [the Albanian security police] plants cache of arms and ammunition in main Franciscan church in Shkodra. When 'discovered' many Franciscan priests and brothers are arrested, tortured, and executed. Among them, their provincial, Father Cyprian Nika. All their schools and monasteries are closed, properties confiscated, and the order disbanded.

February 1948: 44-year-old Bishop of Sappa, Gjergj (George) Volaj is executed after horrible torture.

March 1948: Abbot Frano Gjini, substitute Apostolic Delegate in Albania, is executed after torture and mock trial, along with 17 other clerics and lay people.

February 1949: Metropolitan Archbishop of Durres, author and poet Vincent Prendushi, dies in prison after much torture and suffering.

August 1951: A new wave of persecution washes over the Church. Between 1951 and 1965, dozens of priests and religious are executed, imprisoned, or sent to forced labour camps in Southern Albania. Among these, Fathers Ded (Dominic) Malaj, Zef Bici, Nikol Mazrreku, Andrew Lufi, Tom Laca, Gjon and Engjel Kovaci, Anton Suma, and Konrad Gjolaj.

February 1967: Enver Hoxha orders a final attack to wipe out the Church and all religious activity. In a speech on 6 February 1967, Hoxha urges Albanian youth to fight 'religious superstitions' with all their vigor. A strong anti-religious campaign follows. Churches and mosques everywhere are burned or converted to other uses; priests and bishops are publicly beaten, arrested and sent to prison and labour camps for 're-education'. By the end of the year 2,200 churches, mosques, chapels, and other religious buildings are vandalized and closed.

February 1972: Father Shtjefen (Stephen) Kurti is executed for baptizing a child.

December 1976: The new constitution of Albania officially outlaws religion.

April 1979: The Titular Bishop of Shkodra, Ernest Coba, dies in a labour camp from police beatings for holding an Easter celebration.

May 1980: Father Ndoc Luli, S.J. is sentenced to life in prison for baptizing twins of his own family.

The *Albanian Catholic Bulletin* reported that the forty years of the Albanian government's savage campaign against the Catholic Church resulted in the arrest and death of two archbishops, five bishops, an abbot, 64 diocesan priests, 33 Franciscans, 14 Jesuits, ten seminarians and eight nuns. Their only crime was believing in God and their determination to profess this belief.

Chapter 3

Persecution enters a new era

When the slumbering giants of injustice emerge in the earth,
we need to know that there is a God of power who can cut
them down like the grass . . .

Martin Luther King, Jr

The 1980s saw Christians at the forefront of regime changes in
Eastern Europe. Fr Jerzy Popieluszko's church in Warsaw
became a focal point for the Polish people. As a result of his
stand, Fr Jerzy was martyred. Christian Führer in East Germany
and László Tökés in Romania were also at the heart of the
changes in their countries as thousands converged on their
churches, which became centres for prayer.

I had the opportunity to visit Fr Jerzy's church in Warsaw a
few weeks before he was murdered. I clearly remember the
pervasive atmosphere of tension. The fear was almost tangible.
This is perhaps a reminder that we are all human and that those
facing the possibility of impending martyrdom are not protected from dread. They may also have to endure their Gethsemane experience and, like our Lord, hope and pray that if it is
God's will, the cup which they may be about to drink, might
be taken away from them.

Jerzy Popieluszko (1947–1984), Poland

Poland celebrated 1,000 years of Christianity in 1965. In
response, the Communist government began a sustained anti-
church campaign. It was also the year that Jerzy Popieluszko
began training for the priesthood in Warsaw. A year later he
was drafted into the army and spent the next two years in a

special army indoctrination unit designed to break trainee clerics.

Although he had always been physically frail, he wrote to his father: 'I turned out to be very tough. I can't be broken by threats or torture.'

Popieluszko became the spiritual leader of the unit, leading prayer services, but as a result he was assigned extra hard labour which left his health severely damaged. His Christian faith remained undimmed, however, and he wrote: 'How sweet it is to suffer when you know that you suffer for Christ.'

At the end of his two years of 're-education' Popieluszko was still determined to become a priest and was ordained on 28 May 1972, though frail health forced him to leave parish duties six years later. In June 1980, at the age of 32, he became a resident priest at the church of St Stanislaw Kostka, a position usually reserved for retired priests. However, his new role heralded the start of what was to become the most active part of his life. Two months later the Warsaw steelworkers came out on strike in support of the Gdansk shipyard workers led by Lech Walesa. The steelworkers wanted a priest to celebrate Mass for them and, as St Stanislaw Kostka Church was nearby, they asked Fr Jerzy. After the strike he became an honorary member of the workers' movement Solidarity and agreed to become their chaplain.

From that point he was shadowed by the secret police and received death threats warning him to break contact with Solidarity. On Sunday, 13 December 1981, martial law was declared throughout Poland. Solidarity members were arrested and detained in internment camps; Solidarity's sympathizers were persecuted and all protests were stifled. But Fr Jerzy did not stop speaking out against the injustice he saw.

In an account of Popieluszko's life, Grazyna Sikorski writes:

Fr. Jerzy was the only priest who attended the political show trial of Solidarity activists staged by the government. He saw it simply as an integral part of his ministry: 'The work of a priest is in a way an extension of the work of Christ . . . the duty of a priest is to be with the people when they need him most, when they are wronged, degraded or maltreated. For there is always suffering and pain when basic human rights are not respected, when there is no freedom of speech or opinion, when people are imprisoned for their convictions. And there are so many such people in our country, especially since that December night in 1981. I felt that perhaps it was then that they needed me most, in those difficult times, praying for them in their prison cells, in the court rooms where I went to hear the trials.'[1]

Fr Jerzy sat with the families of the accused during the trials. He also built up an information network to identify who had been detained, together with the names and addresses of their relatives. He created his own welfare system, distributing as much Western aid as he could get. His help was not limited to regular churchgoers. One young mother, reluctant to accept charity, is quoted as saying: 'How can I take help from you? My husband and I aren't believers.' 'That doesn't matter now,' Fr Jerzy answered. 'We are divided only into people who need and people who can give.'

As well as meeting the practical needs of those being persecuted, Fr Jerzy sought to meet spiritual needs, so the 'Mass for the Fatherland' began one month after the imposition of martial law. At the first Mass for the Fatherland Fr Jerzy spoke just one short sentence: 'Because freedom of speech has been taken from us let us pray in silence for those brothers and sisters who have been deprived of their freedom.' Three minutes' silence followed.

After that, crowds flocked to attend the Masses for the Fatherland, held each month. As Fr Jerzy said, 'When people suffer and are persecuted the Church also feels the pain. The mission of the Church is to be with people and to share their joys and sorrows . . . to serve God is to speak about evil as a sickness which should be brought to light so it can be cured. To serve God is to condemn evil in all its manifestations.'[2]

Fr Jerzy was not afraid to speak the truth about what was happening to his country under martial law. He condemned the murder of 19-year-old poet Grzegorz Przemyk by members of the security police in May 1983 and compared the suffering of Poland with the suffering of Christ. He also spoke out against any thoughts of hatred or revenge, and asked people to pray, not only for those who were wronged, but also for those 'who caused human suffering, anxiety, and fear . . . for lawyers, representing justice, who did not have the courage to oppose lies and falsehood . . . for those who violated human conscience'.[3]

The authorities tried to silence Fr Jerzy. His phone was tapped, his home was fire-bombed and his car was sprayed with paint. Writer and broadcaster Mary Craig, who visited him in 1983, asked him if he was afraid. 'Of course I am,' he replied, 'On the human level I'm scared stiff. But if you believe in Christ, you know there's another dimension beyond fear. If they arrest me, even if they go on to torture and kill me, the story won't end there.

'People from all over Poland are writing every day, thanking me for saying what they themselves dare not say. Some of these people are returning to the Church after being away from it for twenty, thirty years. How could I possibly betray them? Even if I am afraid, I can't give up.'[4]

Asked if his life was in danger he told Mary Craig: 'Yes – but it's better to risk violent death in a worthwhile cause than to opt out and let injustice take over.'[5]

In the summer of 1983, the authorities ordered an official investigation into Fr Popieluszko's 'abuse of freedom of conscience and religion'. On 12 December 1983 Jerzy was summoned to the district prosecutor's office, charged with 'storing explosives, firearms and ammunition' which had been 'discovered' after a three-minute search of his flat by police with a camera crew. He spent the night of 12–13 December in a prison cell – holding an all-night conversation with a murderer who by dawn had broken down, confessed and responded to Christ. On his release, Jerzy was warned to behave. He was interrogated thirteen times between January and June 1984 and his flat was mysteriously burned out in September 1984.

The first attempt on Fr Jerzy's life took place on 13 October

1984. He and his driver were travelling on the Gdansk–Warsaw road when a man jumped out and tried to throw something at the car. The driver swerved and the 'accident' was avoided. A week later Fr Popieluszko was invited to celebrate Mass at Bydgoszcz in northern Poland. His theme was 'overcome evil with good'. On the journey home the car was stopped by a traffic policeman. When the driver was arrested, Fr Jerzy protested. Popieluszko was beaten, bound, gagged and thrown into the boot of the police car. His driver succeeded in escaping and alerted the Church authorities.

The body of Jerzy Popieluszko was retrieved ten days later from the Wloclawek Reservoir. His body was covered with wounds. His jaw, nose, mouth and skull were smashed. Part of his scalp and large strips of skin on his legs had been torn off. In the end, it was Fr Jerzy's brother who identified him from a birthmark on his chest. One of the doctors who performed the post-mortem reported that in all his medical practice, he had never seen anyone so mutilated internally.

Fr Jerzy was buried in the churchyard at St Stanislaus Kostka. His grave has been visited by many leading statesmen and in June 1987 Pope John Paul II knelt to pray at the grave of the martyred priest.

Christian Führer (b. 1943), Leipzig, Germany

The turning point for East Germany was prayer. When the Deutsche Demokratische Republik was descending into chaos in the 1980s, Christian Führer, pastor of the Nikolaikirche in Leipzig, committed his church to pray for peace. By 1989 their weekly Monday night prayer meetings were attracting large numbers of people. Even when his congregation in the Nikolaikirche was doubled by members of the State Security Police, he continued to preach, 'Love your enemies!' Christian Führer was determined to maintain his peaceful, prayerful stand in the face of state pressure.

As Führer recalls:

From 8 May 1989, the driveways to the church were blocked by the police . . . The state authorities exerted greater pressure on us to cancel the peace prayers or at least to transfer them to the city limits. Monday after Monday there were arrests or 'temporary detentions' in connection with the peace prayers. Even so, the number of visitors flocking to the church continued to grow to a point where the 2,000 seats were no longer sufficient. Then came the all-deciding 9 October 1989. And what a day it was! . . .
. . . the opening scene had taken place two days before on 7 October . . . On this day, for 10 long hours, uniformed police battered defenceless people who made no attempt to fight back and took them away in trucks. Hundreds of them were locked up in stables in Markkleeberg . . . an article was published in the press saying that it was high time to put an end to what they called 'counter-revolution', if necessary by armed forces. That was the situation on 9 October 1989.

More than 2,000 people left the church, to be welcomed by 10,000 waiting outside with candles in their hands. Führer adds, 'Horst Sindermann, who was a member of the Central Committee of the GDR, said before his death: "We had planned everything. We were prepared for everything. But not for candles and prayers."'[6]

When the Berlin Wall fell on 9 November 1989, the reality of the power of prayer over governments was seen throughout the world.

László Tökés (b. 1952), Timisoara, Romania

Revd László Tökés resisted state and Church pressure to compromise his Christian faith. Efforts to evict him from his church flat helped trigger the Romanian Revolution of 1989, which overthrew Nicolae Ceausescu and spelled the end of the communist era in Romania.

Mark Elliott explains:

In the summer of 1989, Budapest television secretly video-taped an interview with this Reformed pastor [Revd Tökés] which was smuggled out of Romania and broadcast throughout Hungary on July 24. No holds barred, the thirty-seven-year-old Tökés decried Romanian discrimination against ethnic Hungarians, government manipulation of his church's leadership, and state plans to destroy culturally price-less historic urban districts and thousands of peasant villages. Asked about his boldness, despite years of trial and harassment, Tökés replied, 'As a minister, I feel myself responsible for the people, as one of its spiritual leaders . . . This responsibility is all the more heavy as most of my fellow-ministers are silent.'[7]

The leaders of Romania's Hungarian Reformed Church had given in to state pressure and, for years, had been calling on Tökés and his father, Revd István Tökés, to keep quiet. László Tökés had been dismissed by his bishop from one parish, trans-ferred to another church in Timisoara, rebuked by Bishop László Papp for speaking out about state restrictions on the Church and, finally, ordered to a remote village. When Tökés refused to leave Timisoara, Papp attempted to fire him. Parish-ioners rallied to support their pastor.

Elliott continues,

On September 12, Ernö Ujvárossy, a church member strongly supportive [of] Tökés, disappeared, following a barrage of threats to him and his family. His body was discovered in woods outside Timisoara on September 16, amidst strong circumstantial evidence linking the security police to his death. Another loyal parishioner was hospitalized following major head injuries sustained during a police interrogation . . .

. . . Tökés then moved his family into the church proper where on November 2 four masked assailants attacked and stabbed the pastor in the presence of his pregnant wife. Police made no attempt to stop the assault. On audio tape smuggled out of the country, an unnerved Tökés could not hide the effects of the strain: 'They've broken our windows every day,' he reported. 'Now they've started breaking them in the church as well . . . The nights are terrible.'

The fearless stand of Rev. Tökés and his church came to a climax the weekend of December 15–17, and to the amazement of all concerned triggered massive sympathy demonstrations first in Timisoara, then in Bucharest, toppling the Ceausescu regime in a matter of days.

It all started on Friday, December 15, with a moving truck pulling up in front of the parsonage of the Reformed Church of Timisoara. In the words of Peter Dugulescu, pastor of the Timisoara First Baptist Church, 'First the believers from his (Reformed) churches and then, believers from other denominations and many other people . . . came out to support him. The truck remained unloaded . . . Tökés addressed the people from a window, asking them to trust God, to be peaceful . . . The mayor of the town also addressed the people that had gathered (Reformed, Baptist, Catholic, and Orthodox; Hungarian and Romanian) . . . asking them to disperse, but the crowd would not.'

On Saturday evening, December 16, Rev. Dugulescu drove by the Reformed church, meeting Daniel Gavra, a twenty-four-year-old railway worker from his church who told his pastor that he and other young people were there to defend Tökés. He showed me that he brought with him (hidden under his coat) a bundle of candles, and he told me that after it got dark, he was going to distribute them to the young people, to keep them burning in front of Pastor Tökés' house.' Badly wounded in subsequent fighting Gavra had to have a leg amputated. His words to his pastor from his hospital bed were that he had lost a leg but he had lit the first candle.

[That same evening,] the crowds surrounding the Reformed church came under attack by the police and were sprayed with foam and water from fir[e] engines. 'People were running, others were forced into buses and later that evening many were arrested.' Tökés himself was arrested on Sunday, December 17, while about 5:00 p.m. that evening, Dugulescu reports, 'the first shootings were heard in the city . . . In the square between the opera house and the cathedral, people stayed the whole night . . . among them there was a girl from our church near the opera house, and she hid and saw how armed terrorists, dressed in army uniforms, fire[d] machine-guns at the crowds of people.' Afterwards she counted 382 dead bodies between the opera and the cathedral.

. . . in Timisoara, security police loyal to Ceausescu were in retreat . . . army units sided with youthful protestors, confounding forces loyal to the dictator. On Friday, December 22, Rev. Peter Dugulescu was on a balcony overlooking the city's opera square when official word came of the overthrow of Ceausescu . . . the people started to shout, enthusiastically: 'God exists!' 'There is a God.'[8]

Dugulescu said, 'With some 150,000 people in the square, I asked the crowd that in these great, historic and critical moments we should pray together the prayer, "Our father, Who art in Heaven." Without being asked to do it, all of them knelt down, facing the cathedral I prayed in the microphone, and they repeated after me. What I had realized was that throughout the manifestations in Timisoara, there was a strong religious accent, after so many years of atheistic education that was systematically carried out among the youth, and people. This shout, this hunger for God burst strongly several times a day – about five times – they would pray together this prayer and would shout: "God exists."'[9]

László Tökés became bishop of the Hungarian Reformed Church in Transylvania, Romania. Peter Dugulescu became a member of the Romanian parliament. Their action in the face of persecution was a catalyst for change.

Chapter 4

Persecution in Britain –
the price of conversion to
Christianity from Islam in
contemporary Britain

Foxe's Book of Martyrs – the sixteenth-century classic which inspired this volume – includes two chapters on persecution in Britain: an account of persecution in Scotland during the reign of Henry VIII and a substantial chapter on persecution in England during Queen Mary's reign.

The most severe and systematic forms of persecution today are found in parts of the world featured in the preceding chapters. But lest those of us who live in what we call 'the West' should think that no one in our midst is suffering for their faith, we end with a reminder that there are those in countries such as Britain who are paying a high price for their faith.

These examples of attacks on citizens should not be confused with other kinds of assault, such as racially motivated crimes – although those are also appalling and abhorrent. But the violence described in these cases is distinctive because it is inflicted in response to a deliberate choice made by the victims: the choice to change their faith. Moreover, these people know the consequences which are likely to follow – not only for themselves, but also for their families.

Although adherents of some faiths may exercise understandable pressure on their families and communities not to convert to other religions or to marry those of other faiths (or none), they do not practise systematic violence against those who do. However, there are traditions within Islam which teach that those who convert to other faiths are guilty of apostasy, which may incur the ultimate penalty. Also, in some traditions,

Muslims who marry non-Muslims may expect to suffer severe reprisals.

In March 2005 the cover of the *Spectator* pictured a cross with the headline: 'Why Christians are still persecuted'. The corresponding feature by Anthony Browne, entitled 'Church of Martyrs', claimed that more than 300 million Christians were either threatened with violence or legally discriminated against because of their faith.

In his role as Europe correspondent of *The Times*, Browne had uncovered stories of severe persecution and suspected murder – not in some far-flung dictatorship but in Britain. In *The Times* on 5 February 2005, he had written:

> The first brick was thrown through the sitting room window at one in the morning, waking Nissar Hussein, his wife and five children with a terrifying start. The second brick went through his car window.
>
> It was a shock, but hardly a surprise. The week before, another brick had been thrown through the window as the family were preparing for bed in their Bradford home. The victim of a three-year campaign of religious hatred, Mr Hussein's car has also been rammed and torched, and the steps to his home have been strewn with rubbish.
>
> He and his family have been regularly jostled, abused, attacked, shouted at to move out of the area, and given death threats in the street. His wife has been held hostage inside their home for two hours by a mob. His car, walls and windows have been daubed in graffiti: 'Christian bastard'.

Browne's article in *The Times* included other stories of British Christians persecuted for their faith. Yasmin converted from Islam after having a vision of Jesus when she gave birth to her youngest son. She was baptized in her thirties, but told Browne:

> My family completely disowned me. They thought I had committed the biggest sin – I was born a Muslim, and so I must die a Muslim. When my husband found out, he totally

disowned my sons. One friend tried to strangle me when I told him I was converting. We had bricks through our windows, I was spat at in the street because they thought I was dishonouring Islam. We had to call the police so many times. I had to go to court to get an injunction against my husband because he was inciting others to attack me.

Yasmin and other converts from Islam have set up support groups across England for converts from Islam. They meet in secret and have to vet those who approach them for fear of infiltrators.

'There are so many who convert from Islam to Christianity. We have 70 people on our list whom we support, and the list is growing. We don't want others to suffer like we have,' Yasmin told Browne.

When the family of one 18-year-old girl whom Yasmin was helping found that she had been hiding a Bible in her room and visiting church secretly, they took her to Pakistan 'on holiday'. 'Three weeks later, she was drowned – they said that she went out in the middle of the night and slipped in the river, but she just wouldn't have done that,' Yasmin told Browne.

Ruth, of Pakistani origin, also featured in Browne's *Times* article. When she told her family that she had converted, they kept her locked inside the family home all summer. 'They were afraid I would meet some Christians. My brother was aggressive, and even hit me – I later found out he wanted me dead,' she said. A family friend had suggested taking her to Pakistan to kill her, and her brother put the idea to her mother, who ruled against it. 'You are very isolated and very alone,' said Ruth. 'But now, my brother is thinking about changing and a cousin has made a commitment to Christianity.'

Noor, from the Midlands, converted from Islam to Christianity at 21. 'Telling my father was the most difficult thing I have ever done. I thought he would kill me on the spot, but he just went into a state of shock,' she told Browne. Noor's father took drastic action, she said: 'He took the family to Pakistan, to a secluded village with no roads to it. He kept us there for many years, putting pressure on me to leave my Christian faith.

I endured mental and emotional suffering that most humans never reach.' When her father realized that her Christian faith could not be shaken, he released her, but she lives under strict conditions.

In the *Spectator* article, Anthony Browne commented, 'Although persecution of Christians is greatest in Muslim countries, it happens in countries of all religions and none.'

Browne quoted Dr Paul Marshall, senior fellow at the Centre for Religious Freedom in Washington, DC, who estimates that there are 200 million Christians who face violence because of their faith, and 350 million who face legally sanctioned discrimination in terms of access to jobs and housing. The World Evangelical Alliance wrote in a report to the UN Human Rights Commission in 2004 that Christians are 'the largest single group in the world which is being denied human rights on the basis of their faith'.

'As a liberal democrat atheist, I believe all persecuted people should be helped equally, irrespective of their religion,' Browne concluded, 'But the guilt-ridden West is ignoring people because of their religion. If non-Christians like me can sense the nonsense, how does it make Christians feel? And how are they going to react?'

Dr Patrick Sookhdeo, director of the Barnabas Trust, which helps persecuted Christians, has told me the situation for Britain's Christian converts from Islam is worsening. Some church leaders who are seeking good interfaith relationships have announced that their churches cannot receive converts from Islam. 'Leaders like the Bishop of Bradford are sacrificing converts on the altar of good relationships with other faiths,' Dr Sookhdeo explained. Meanwhile, he added, some of those converts have been kidnapped, beaten and threatened with death, but 'The response from the police is generally that they don't want to be involved.'

Nissar Hussein, Yasmin, Ruth, Noor and others like them follow in a long line of persecuted Christians which can be traced back to Jesus himself. As Jesus said, 'Remember the words I spoke to you: "No servant is greater than his master." If they persecuted me, they will persecute you also' (John 15:20).

Epilogue

T. S. Eliot, 'Choruses from "The Rock"' VI

It is hard for those who have never known persecution,
And who have never known a Christian,
To believe these tales of Christian persecution.
It is hard for those who live near a Bank
To doubt the security of their money.
It is hard for those who live near a Police Station
To believe in the triumph of violence.
Do you think that the Faith has conquered the World
And that lions no longer need keepers? –
Do you need to be told that whatever has been, can still be?
Do you need to be told that even such modest attainments
As you can boast in the way of polite society
Will hardly survive the Faith to which they owe their significance?
Men! polish your teeth on rising and retiring;
Women! polish your fingernails:
You polish the tooth of the dog and the talon of the cat.
Why should men love the Church? Why should they love her laws?
She tells them of Life and Death, and of all that they would forget.
She is tender where they would be hard, and hard where they like to be soft.
She tells them of Evil and Sin, and other unpleasant facts.
They constantly try to escape
From the darkness outside and within
By dreaming of systems so perfect that no one will need to be good.
But the man that is will shadow

Epilogue

The man that pretends to be.
And the Son of Man was not crucified once for all,
The blood of the martyrs not shed once for all,
The lives of the Saints not given once for all:
But the Son of Man is crucified always
And there shall be Martyrs and Saints.[1]

Notes

Part I

Chapter 4

1 Desmond Tutu with Douglas Abrams, *God has a Dream: A Vision of Hope For Our Time* (London: Rider, 2004), p. 2.
2 Ibid., pp. 3–4

Chapter 5

1 Ayub Masih, 'Death Sentence', available at <www.jubileeaction.co.uk/justright/spring2004_article1.html> (accessed 23 January 2006).

Part II

Chapter 1

1 Quoted in 'Allen Yuan Exchanges his Cross for a Crown', available at <www.persecution.net/news/china84a.html> (accessed 23 January 2006).
2 Brother David with Sara Bruce and Lela Gilbert, *Walking the Hard Road: The Wang Ming-Tao Story* (London: Marshall Pickering, 1989), pp. 92–93.
3 Newman Sze, *The Martyrdom of Watchman Nee* (Culver City, Calif.: Testimony Publications, 1997), p. 67.
4 'Watchman Nee's Life and Ministry', sect. 8 ('Martyrdom'), available at <www.watchmannee.org/life-ministry.html> (accessed 15 January 2006).

Chapter 3

1 'Testimony of Soon Ok Lee, April 30, 2003, House Committee on International Relations', available at <www.house.gov/internationalrelations/108/lee0430.htm> (accessed 13 January 2006).

Chapter 4

1 Cardinal François Xavier Nguyen Van Thuan, 'Cardinal Nguyen Van Thuan (1928–2002): How Faith Survived in a Communist Prison', available at <www.ad2000.com.au/articles/2003/may2003p10_1322.html> (accessed 13 January 2006).
2 'Death of Cardinal Nguyen Van Thuan', available at <www.cathnews.com/news/209/103.php> (accessed 13 January 2006).

Notes

Part III

Chapter 1

1 Elizabeth Roberts and Ann Shukman (eds), *Christianity for the Twenty-First Century: The Life and Work of Alexander Men* (London: SCM Press, 1996), pp. 12, 15.

2 Georgi Vins, *Three Generations of Suffering* (London: Hodder & Stoughton, 1976), p. 217.

Chapter 2

1 Quoted in Georgi Vins, *Three Generations of Suffering* (London: Hodder & Stoughton, 1976), pp. 31–32.

2 Michael Bourdeaux, *Faith on Trial in Russia* (London: Hodder & Stoughton, 1971), p. 101.

3 Quotations from the trial transcript are taken from Bourdeaux, *Faith on Trial in Russia*, pp. 126–30.

4 Ibid., pp. 131–32.

Chapter 3

1 Trevor Beeson, *Rebels and Reformers* (London: SCM Press, 1999), p. 134.

2 All of the information in the following biographies is taken from *Religion in Communist Lands*, 11:1 (Spring 1983), pp. 83–88.

Chapter 4

1 Caroline Cox and John Eibner, *Ethnic Cleansing in Progress: War in Nagorno Karabakh*, with a preface by Elena Bonner Sakharov (Zurich and London: Institute for Religious Minorities in the Islamic World, 1993).

Chapter 5

1 Christmas meditation at <home.earthlink.net/~amenpage/christian_hope.htm> (accessed 16 March 2006).

2 Elizabeth Roberts and Ann Shukman (eds), *Christianity for the Twenty-First Century: The Life and Work of Alexander Men* (London: SCM Press, 1996), p. 11.

3 Ibid., p. 17.

Part IV

Chapter 4

1 'Rescue the Future of Sudan', available at <www.eglisesoudan.org/docbish/02.htm> (accessed 4 January 2006).

Chapter 5

1 Frederick Quinn, *African Saints: Saints, Martyrs, and Holy People From the Continent of Africa* (New York: Crossroad Publishing Co., 2002); quoted in 'Festo Kivengere', available at <www.dacb.org/stories/uganda/kivengere_festo.html> (accessed 23 January 2006).

Notes

2 Mary Craig, *Candles in the Dark: Six Modern Martyrs* (London: Hodder & Stoughton, 1984), pp. 170–71.
3 Ibid.

Part V
Chapter 1

1 Diana Dewar, *All for Christ: Some Twentieth-Century Martyrs* (Oxford: Oxford University Press, 1980), p. 45.
2 Dora Tenenoff, 'There Once was a Man . . .', available at <www.pastor-swife.net/hostage.htm> (accessed 15 January 2006).
3 Quoted in 'Oscar Arnulfo Romero: Prophet to the Americas', available at <www.rtfcam.org/martyrs/romero/romero.htm> (accessed 15 January 2006).
4 'Advent & Christmas Reflections from Oscar Romero', available at <www.beyondborders.net/Christmas/Romero-Advent.htm> (accessed 15 January 2006).

Part VI
Chapter 1

1 See Ann Elizabeth Mayer, *Islam and Human Rights: Tradition and Politics*, 3rd edn (Boulder, Colo. and Oxford: Westview Press, 1999), and Caroline Cox and John Marks, *The 'West', Islam and Islamism: Is Ideological Islam Compatible with Liberal Democracy* (London: Institute for the Study of Civil Society, 2003).
2 Quoted in Jeff M. Sellers, 'How to Confront a Theocracy', *Christianity Today*, 46:8 (8 July 2002), p. 34.

Chapter 2

1 'Text of the Draft Iraqi Constitution', available at <www.news.bbc.co.uk/1/shared/bsp/hi/pdfs/24_08_05_constit.pdf> (accessed 23 January 2006).
2 Ibid.
3 David Thomas, 'Onward Christian Soldier', *Daily Telegraph*, 14 June 2005.
4 Andrew White, 'News From Canon Andrew White and the Iraq Mission', available at <www.ecusa-chaplain.org/Canon_Andrew_White.Mission.htm> (accessed 15 January 2006).

Chapter 3

1 Bernard Lewis, *The Political Language of Islam* (Chicago: University of Chicago Press, 1988), p. 72.

Chapter 4

1 'The Written Defense of the Rev. Mehdi Dibaj Delivered to the Sari Court of Justice', available at <www.farsinet.com/dibaj/index.html> (accessed 15 January 2006).

Notes

Part VII

Chapter 1

1 Mary Craig, *Candles in the Dark: Six Modern Martyrs* (London: Hodder & Stoughton, 1984), p. 39.
2 Ibid., 51.
3 Ibid., 55.
4 Ibid.
5 Ibid., pp. 57–58.
6 Ibid., p. 59.
7 'History', available at <www.corrietenbom.com/history.htm> (accessed 16 January 2006).
8 Corrie ten Boom, *The Hiding Place*, 4th edn (London: Hodder & Stoughton, 2004) p. 202.
9 Ibid., 220–21.

Chapter 2

1 'Persecution of Catholics in Albania', *Albanian Catholic Bulletin*, 6 (1985), available at <www.cin.org/users/msmith/persecution/albania/albania1.html> (accessed 16 January 2006).

Chapter 3

1 Grazyna Sikorski, *Jerzy Popieluszko: Victim of Communism* (London: Catholic Truth Society, 1999), p. 24.
2 Ibid., p. 32.
3 Ibid.
4 Mary Craig, *Candles in the Dark: Six Modern Martyrs* (London: Hodder & Stoughton, 1984), p. 275.
5 Ibid.
6 Quotations from Christian Führer, 'The Events in Fall 1989', at <www.nikolaikirche-leipzig.de/e/the_events_in_fall_1989/the_events_in_fall_1989.html> (accessed 16 January 2006).
7 Mark Elliott, 'Laszlo Tökés, Timisoara and the Romanian Revolution', *Religion in Eastern Europe*, 10:5 (October 1990), pp. 22–28.
8 Ibid.
9 Ibid., p. 28.

Epilogue

1 T. S. Eliot, 'Choruses from the Rock', VI, in *Collected Poems 1909–1962* (London: Faber & Faber Ltd, 1963), p. 174.

Further resources

Aid to the Church in Need

Aid to the Church in Need (ACN) is a Roman Catholic charity supporting 7,000 projects every year throughout the world and publishing reports on the persecuted Church (see Further Reading below). Postal address: ACN-USA, 725 Leonard St, PO Box 220384, Brooklyn, NY11222, USA. Website: <www.aidforthechurchinneed.org>. E-mail: ACN UK: <acn@acnuk.org>; USA: <acnusa@aol.com>.

Assist News Service

The Assist News Service is an international ministry founded by journalist and author Dan Wooding and his wife Norma. It carries regular reports on the persecuted Church around the world. Postal address: Assist News Service, PO Box 609, Lake Forest, CA 92609-0609, USA. Website: <www.assist-news.net>. E-mail: <danjuma1@aol.com>.

Barnabas Fund

Barnabas Fund was established in 1993 and serves the suffering Church and makes their needs known to Christians around the world, encouraging them to pray. It provides practical help to strengthen and encourage the Church in many different ways. It also channels aid to projects run by national Christians in more than 40 countries. Postal address: Barnabas Fund, The Old Rectory, River Street, Pewsey, Wiltshire SN9 5DB, UK. Website: <www.barnabas-fund.org>. E-mail: <info@barnabasfund.org>.

Compass Direct

Compass Direct is a Christian news agency that reports exclusively on Christian persecution around the world. Postal address: Compass Direct News Service, PO Box 27250, Santa Ana, CA 92799, USA. Website: <www.compassdirect.org>. E-mail: <info@compassdirect.org>.

CSW

CSW (Christian Solidarity Worldwide) is an advocacy organization speaking on behalf of the persecuted Church. Postal address: CSW, PO Box 99, New Malden, Surrey KT3 3YF. Website: <www.csw.org.uk>. E-mail: <admin@csw.org.uk>.

Further resources

Elam Ministries

The mission of Elam Ministries is to strengthen and expand the Church in Iran and beyond. With this in mind, Elam trains Christians from the Iran region; equips leaders and workers with resources and opportunities that will assist them; and sends people to strengthen existing churches and to establish new churches. Postal address: Elam Ministries UK, PO Box 75, Godalming, Surrey GU8 6YP, UK or Elam Ministries USA, 1000 Abbey Court, Alpharetta, GA 30004, USA. Website: <www.elam.com>. For e-mail contact, visit their website.

HART

HART (Humanitarian Aid Relief Trust) is a humanitarian aid organization founded by Baroness Cox. It focuses primarily on 'forgotten people in forgotten lands' – those who are, or who have recently been, suffering oppression and persecution and who are not being served by the major relief organizations. Postal address: HART, 3 Arnellan House, 146 Slough Lane, Kingsbury, London NW9 8XJ, UK; American Friends of HART, PO Box 18613, Irvine, CA 92623, USA. Website: <www.hart-uk.org>. E-mail: <office@hart-uk.org>.

Jubilee Campaign

Jubilee Campaign is a human rights pressure group, lobbying to protect children's rights and the persecuted Church. It specializes in running targeted campaigns which aim to challenge authorities to change unjust laws and serve as a voice for Christians, and for children who are treated unjustly. Postal address: Jubilee Campaign, St Johns, Cranleigh Road, Wonersh, Guildford, Surrey GU5 0QX, UK. Website: <www.jubileecampaign.co.uk>. E-mail: <info@jubileecampaign.co.uk>.

Keston Institute

Monitors freedom of religion and researches religious affairs in communist and post-communist countries. Postal address: Keston Institute, 38 St Aldates, Oxford OX1 1BN, UK. Website: <www.keston.org>. E-mail: <keston.institute@keston.org>.

Open Doors

Open Doors has been serving and strengthening persecuted Christians since 1955, when its founder Brother Andrew, author of *God's Smuggler*, slipped behind the Iron Curtain to strengthen, encourage and bring God's word to suffering believers. Open Doors now works in 45 countries across the world. Postal address: Open Doors UK, PO Box 6, Witney, Oxon. OX29 6WG, UK. Website: <www.opendoorsuk.org>. E-mail: <info@opendoorsuk.org>.

Further reading

Bold as a Lamb: Pastor Samuel Lamb and the Underground Church of China, by Ken Anderson (Zondervan, 1991).

Candles in the Dark: Six Modern Martyrs, by Mary Craig (Hodder & Stoughton, 1984).

Christianity for the Twenty-First Century, ed. Elizabeth Roberts and Ann Shukman (SCM Press, 1996).

The Cross and the Crescent: Religious Freedom in Countries with an Islamic Majority, by Andrea Morigi, Vittorio Emanuele Vernole and Priscilla di Thiene (Aid to the Church in Need, 2000).

Ethnic Cleansing in Progress: War in Nagorno Karabakh, by Caroline Cox and John Eibner (Institute for Religious Minorities in the Islamic World, 1993).

Eyes of the Tailless Animals, by Soon Ok Lee (Living Sacrifice Book Co., 1999).

Faith on Trial in Russia, by Michael Bourdeaux (Hodder and Stoughton, 1971).

Foxe's Book of Martyrs, by John Foxe (Henrickson Publishers, 2004).

Jerzy Popieluszko: Victim of Communism, by Grazyna Sikorski (Catholic Truth Society, 1999).

A Living Sacrifice: The Life Story of Allen Yuan, by Lydia Lee (Sovereign World, 2001).

The Long Road to Freedom: The Story of Wang Mingdao, by Stephen Wang (Sovereign World, 2002).

Religion in Communist Lands (published by the Centre for the Study of Religion and Communism, 1973–91).

Religious Ferment in Russia, by Michael Bourdeaux (Macmillan, 1968).

Their Blood Cries Out: The Untold Story of Persecution against Christians in the Modern World, by Paul Marshall with Lela Gilbert (World Publishing, 1997).

Three Generations of Suffering, by Georgi Vins (Hodder & Stoughton, 1976).

Walking the Hard Road, by Brother David with Lela Gilbert (Open Doors International, 1989).

Index of Places

Index of People

Index of People

Baroness Cox of Queensbury

Baroness (Caroline) Cox was created a Life Peer in 1982 and was a deputy speaker of the House of Lords from 1985 to 2005. She was Founder Chancellor of Bournemouth University (1991–2001) and is a Vice-President of the Royal College of Nursing. She has been heavily involved with international humanitarian work, serving as a non-executive director of the Andrei Sakharov Foundation; as a trustee of Merlin (Medical Emergency Relief International); as an honorary member of the Council of the Siberian medical University in Tomsk; and as Chief Executive of HART (Humanitarian Aid Relief Trust).

Lady Cox has been honoured with the Commander Cross of the Order of Merit of the Republic of Poland and the Wilberforce Award for her humanitarian work; she received the anniversary medal presented by Lech Walesa, the former President of Poland, at the twenty-fifth anniversary of the Polish Solidarity Movement (October 2005); and the President of the Republic of Armenia conferred on her the Mkhitar Gosh Medal (September 2005). She has also been awarded an Honorary Fellowship of the Royal College of Surgeons of England and honorary doctorates by universities in the United Kingdom, the United States of America, the Russian federation, and Armenia.

Baroness Cox's work in the field of humanitarian aid has taken her on many missions to areas of conflict, including the Armenian enclave of Nagorno Karabakh; war zones in Africa, including Sudan and Nigeria; the Karen, Karenni and Chin peoples in the jungles of Burma; and communities suffering from intercommunal fighting in Indonesia. She has visited North Korea to promote parliamentary initiatives and medical programmes. She has also been instrumental in helping to change the former Soviet Union's policies for orphaned and abandoned children from institutional to foster family care.

In 2004 she was appointed as Special Representative for the Foreign and Commonwealth Office Freedom of Religion Panel.

Catherine Butcher

Catherine Butcher has worked as a journalist, writer and editor since graduating in Government and Modern History in 1981. Current affairs has been a lifelong interest but her passion has always been to bring faith-building stories of the unsung to a wider audience. The stories of Christians she has met from Eritrea, Romania, Israel and China have fuelled her interest in the plight of Christians living with persecution around the world.

Catherine trained as a newspaper journalist and has focused on magazine feature-writing while editing a number of local, national and international publications. She has edited the Bible Reading Fellowship's devotional series *Day by Day with God* since 2003 and has also written several books.

As well as writing during home-based years with her children, she has chaired a local charity, run a women's breakfast club and served as a school governor. She gained a Master's degree in Spirituality from the University of London in 2005.